MULTIMEDIA INFORMATION SYSTEMS

edited by

V. S. Subrahmanian
University of Maryland

Satish K. Tripathi
University of California, Riverside

A Special Issue of
MULTIMEDIA TOOLS AND APPLICATIONS
An International Journal

Volume 7, Nos. 1/2 (1998)

KLUWER ACADEMIC PUBLISHERS
Boston / Dordrecht / London

MULTIMEDIA TOOLS AND APPLICATIONS

An International Journal

Volume 7, Nos. 1/2, July 1998

Special Issue: Multimedia Information Systems
Guest Editors: V.S. Subrahmanian and Satish K. Tripathi

Distributors for North, Central and South America:
Kluwer Academic Publishers
101 Philip Drive
Assinippi Park
Norwell, Massachusetts 02061 USA

Distributors for all other countries:
Kluwer Academic Publishers
Distribution Centre
Post Office Box 322
3300 AH Dordrecht, THE NETHERLANDS

ISBN 978-1-4419-5042-0   e-ISBN 978-0-585-33820-0

Library of Congress Cataloging-in-Publication Data

A C.I.P. Catalogue record for this book is available
from the Library of Congress.

Printed on acid-free paper.

Multimedia Tools and Applications, 7, 5–7 (1998)
© 1998 Kluwer Academic Publishers, Boston.

Guest Editorial

This special issue of *Multimedia Tools and Applications* journal consists of extended versions of a few, selected papers from the 1996 International Workshop on Multimedia Information Systems held at West Point, NY, September 26-28, 1996. This is the second in a series of workshops on multimedia information systems, funded by the US Army Research Office and the University of Maryland Institute for Advanced Computer Studies. The first was held in September 1995, in Arlington, VA.

Research in multimedia involves collaborative and cooperative research from many subareas of computer science: database, knowledgebase, operating systems, and computer networking are a few topics that constitutes the foundation of multimedia systems. Not only must research problems in each of these areas be addressed, the integration of these different solutions is also required before a realistic multimedia database system can be deployed.

For example, in the area of Multimedia Databases, there is a critical need for preprocessing the multimedia information by generating annotations (automatic/semiautomatic), storing the annotations along with the raw data and integration of annotations from different media streams. In multimedia query processing, there is a need for incorporation of approximate matching along with interactive and probabilistic retrieval of information. Indexing different media of information such as the many dimensions involved (temporal, spatial, etc) is also critical. In addition, topics such as Content-Based Query Processing, Content-Based Navigation and Matching, Content Extraction/Annotation, require the seamless integration of image/video/text processing and database technology.

In the area of Networks/OS For Multimedia, there is a need for translating end-to-end QoS to hop-by-hop QoS requirements that need to be available or enforced. The task of determining the QoS requirements for a multimedia application is also important. Rate-based and delay-based resource reservation schemes need to be developed, and I/O schemes need to be restructured to handle multimedia applications. There is also a need for providing uniform I/O abstraction. Security issues, especially the need for an end-to-end view of security, also need to be addressed.

The workshop discussed these topics in great detail. At the end of the workshop, all authors of papers presented at the workshop were invited to submit full length articles for possible publication in this special issue of *Multimedia Tools and Applications* journal. These papers were subjected to a rigorous refereeing process and finally, six papers have been selected for publication in this special issue.

The editors are grateful to the US Army Research Office and the University of Maryland Institute for Advanced Computer Studies for funding the workshop, to the US Military Academy in West Point for graciously hosting the workshop, and to all the researchers and reviewers who graciously participated in the workshop's technical program.

V.S. Subrahmanian
Satish K. Tripathi

Dr. Satish K. Tripathi was born in the village Patna, District Faizabad (UP) on January 20, 1951. He attended the Banaras Hindu University and completed his B.Sc. and M.Sc. (Statistics) in 1968 and 1970, respectively. He stood first in both B.Sc. and M.Sc. in the university and obtained gold medals. He then joined the Indian Statistical Institute, Calcutta to do research in computer science.

In 1972, he left for Canada for higher studies and attended the University of Alberta and the University of Toronto, obtaining Ph.D. in computer Science from the University of Toronto. Dr. Tripathi joined the Computer Science faculty at the University of Maryland in 1978. He served as the Department Chair from 1988-1995. In March 1997, Dr. Tripathi joined the University of California at Riverside as the Dean of Engineering and the Johnson Professor Engineering.

For the last twenty years Dr. Tripathi has been actively involved in research related to performance evaluation, networks, real-time systems and fault tolerance. He has more than one hundred papers in international journals and refereed conferences. In the networking area his current projects are on mobile computing, ATM networks, and operating systems support for multimedia information. He has supervised more than 15 Ph.D. dissertations. Dr. Tripathi has served as the member of the Program Committee and Program Chairman for various international conferences. He has guest edited special issues of many journals and serves on the editorial boards of Theoretical Computer Science, ACM/Springer Multimedia Systems, IEEE/ACM Transactions on Networking, International Journal of High Speed Networking, and IEEE Transactions on Computers. He has edited books in the areas of performance evaluation and parallel computing. Dr. Tripathi is a Fellow of IEEE.

V.S. Subrahmanian received his Ph.D. in Computer Science from Syracuse University in 1989. Since then, he has been on the faculty of the Computer Science Department at the University of Maryland, College Park, where he currently holds the rank of Associate Professor. He received the NSF Young Investigator Award in 1993 and the Distinguished Young Scientist Award from the Maryland Academy of Science in 1997.

He has worked extensively in knowledge bases, bringing together techniques in artificial intelligence and databases. In particular, his work in the area of non-monotonic deductive databases where he proposed well received declarative semantics, as well as efficient implementation paradigms has been influential. He has also worked extensively in the handling of uncertainty in deductive databases, showing how fuzzy and probabilistic data may be neatly manipulated. Finally, he has worked extensively on multimedia systems, and made fundamental contributions to scalable implementation of such systems. More recently, he has been working the problem of integrated heterogeneous data and software located across the Internet. He has proposed formal theoretical models for such inetegrations, as well as led the HERMES project for heterogeneous reasoning and mediator systems. Other implementation efforts he has led include multimedia projects such as MACS for media data, AVIS (for video data), and CHIMP for collaborative multimedia document presentation and authoring.

Prof. Subrahmanian has over 100 published/accepted papers, including ones in prestigious journals such as Journal of the ACM, the ACM Trans. on Databases, IEEE Trans. on Knowledge and Data Engineering, Information and Computation, etc. He has edited two books, one on nonmonotonic reasoning (MIT Press) and one on multimedia databases (Springer). He has co-authored and advanced database textbook (Morgan Kaufman, 1997), and is currently finishing a textbook on multimedia databases (Morgan Kaufman, Jan. 1998). He has given invited talks and served on invited panels at various conferences. In addition, he has served on the program committees of various conferences. He is on the editorial board of IEEE Transactions on Knowledge and Data Engineering and AI Communications. He serves on DARPA's Executive Advisory Council for the Advanced Logistics Program.

Multimedia Tools and Applications, 7, 9–36 (1998)

An Approach to a Content-Based Retrieval of Multimedia Data

GIUSEPPE AMATO   g.amato@iei.pi.cnr.it

Istituto di Elaborazione della Informazione del C.N.R.,
Via S. Maria, 46 - I-56126 Pisa - Italy

GIOVANNI MAINETTO   g.mainetto@cnuce.cnr.it

Istituto CNUCE del C.N.R.,
Via S. Maria, 36 - I-56126 Pisa - Italy

PASQUALE SAVINO   p.savino@iei.pi.cnr.it

Istituto di Elaborazione della Informazione del C.N.R.,
Via S. Maria, 46 - I-56126 Pisa - Italy

Abstract. This paper presents a data model tailored for multimedia data representation, along with the main characteristics of a Multimedia Query Language that exploits the features of the proposed model. The model addresses data presentation, manipulation and content-based retrieval. It consists of three parts: a Multimedia Description Model, which provides a structural view of raw multimedia data, a Multimedia Presentation Model, and a Multimedia Interpretation Model which allows semantic information to be associated with multimedia data. The paper focuses on the structuring of a *multimedia data model* which provides support for content-based retrieval of multimedia data. The Query Language is an extension of a traditional query language which allows restrictions to be expressed on features, concepts, and the structural aspects of the objects of multimedia data and the formulation of queries with imprecise conditions. The result of a query is an approximate set of database objects which partially match such a query.

Keywords: multimedia information systems, information storage and retrieval, data modeling

1. Introduction

In the sixties, both the necessity of managing the large amount of persistent data needed by business applications and the continuous improvements in disk technology led to the definition of simple data models and made the development of Database Systems (DSs) realistic. In the eighties, the need to supply CAD/CAM, VLSI, CASE applications with repositories storing complex structured data, and the possibility to distribute the computational burden on LAN based client-server architectures determined the development of Object-Oriented data models and Object-Oriented DSs. Today, the fact that there are repositories containing huge amounts of multimedia data such as raster images, text documents, video data, scientific data, and the improvement in several technologies that include large capacity storage devices (e.g., CD-Roms, juke-box, disk-array) means that a multimedia data model and architectures designed that are well-suited for Multi Media Database Systems (MMDSs) need to be defined. MMDSs are essential in many new application areas such as merchandising, education, journalism, and television [6, 21]. The provision of MMDSs involves a wide spectrum of fundamental issues in a DS, ranging from access methods and operating system support, efficient multimedia query languages capable of expressing spatial-temporal concepts, sophisticated user interfaces, etc..

This article focuses on the structuring of a *multimedia data model* that provides support for content-based retrieval of multimedia data and the *query language* that exploits such a data model.

The model consists of three parts: a *Multimedia Description Model* (MDM), which provides a structural view of raw multimedia data; a *Multimedia Presentation Model* (MPM), whose main feature is the possibility to describe the temporal and spatial relationships among different structured multimedia data and the *Multimedia Interpretation Model* (MIM) that allows semantic interpretations to be associated with structured multimedia data.

The *Multimedia Presentation Model* is not described in this paper, but is mentioned here for sake of completeness. The problem of presenting of multimedia objects, above all in terms of their presentation and synchronization, has already been addressed in [28, 21, 22]. The emphasis of all these works is on presentation issues, whereas we will discuss the support that the model provides for the retrieval by content of multimedia objects: our presentation is thus limited to MDM and MIM.

The Query Language is an extension of a traditional query language which allows the formulation of interrogations that can simultaneously consider restrictions on features, concepts, and the structural aspects of MMDS objects.

The paper is organized as follows. Section 2 overviews some of the existing approaches. Section 3 gives a general description of our approach for retrieving multimedia data, along with the relations with the proposed model, which is presented in detail in Section 4. The Query Language, which exploits the features offered by the model, is illustrated in Section 5, while Section 6 provides an example of the use of the model and of the Query Language. The final section summarizes the paper and outlines some open issues and areas for future research.

2. Related approaches

Content-based retrieval of multimedia information has been investigated in several research projects. Initial attempts, addressing the problem of retrieval of images, are dated back to the beginning of 80's [11], while from the beginning of 90's the problem of video retrieval has attracted much more attention.

In terms of the information used to represent the content of multimedia data, we can broadly classify the various approaches into three categories [23]:

keyword based, where the content of the multimedia data is described through annotations provided by users such as free text or keywords taken from a controlled vocabulary;

feature based, where a set of features is directly *extracted*, i.e., computed, from the machine readable representation of multimedia data and used for retrieval. Typical features are values that represent either general information, such as *color, texture, shape, speed, position, motion, etc.* or are specific for a particular application, such as *face recognition, trademarks* [40], and *medical images* [33]. Feature extraction is either performed through the supervision and support of the user, or automatically. The latter is in some cases computationally expensive and domain specific.

concept based, where application domain knowledge is used to interpret an object's content. This interpretation leads to the recognition of *concepts* which are used to retrieve the object itself. Usually this process is application domain specific and may require user intervention.

Systems in the first category are based on a manual classification of multimedia objects. Extracted keywords are managed through a conventional Data Base Management System, which provides support for object retrieval.

In the second category are commercial systems such as QBIC [19], Virage [3], and experimental systems such as Photobook [32], VisualSeek [39] and systems for specific application domains, such as medical information systems, face recognition, and trademark management.

QBIC. The QBIC project [19] concentrates on a "nonsemantic" content-based retrieval of pictorial and video databases. The representation of image content is performed on the entire image and on image components. The objects are identified by means of an interaction with the user. Global features are *color histogram, global texture,* and average values of *color distribution.* Object features include *color, texture,* and *shape.* The features associated with shapes are their *area, circularity, eccentricity, axis-orientation,* and *algebraic moment invariant.*

Queries can be formulated through *full scene queries,* which are based on global features, and by using *image prototypes* in order to express restrictions on objects (e.g., *retrieve all images with an object "like this").*

The retrieval is performed by measuring the similarity between the query and the database images. Specific similarity functions are defined for each feature.

Video data are separated into shots, which consist of sets of contiguous frames. Each shot is represented by an *r-frame* which is treated as a still image: features are extracted and stored in the database. Moving objects (e.g., a man running) are extracted from the video.

Systems and approaches that belong to the third category are OVID [31], CORE [40], Infoscopes [26], SCORE [1], Marcus and Subrahamanian [29], and those based on the work of Yoshitaka et al. [41].

OVID. The OVID video database system [31] uses a schemaless approach based on so-called "video objects" (VOs) represented by a tuple-structured value, where references to other VOs can also be present. A partial order (*is-a* hierarchy) is defined over the set of atomic values. The VideoSQL query language allows for the retrieval of video objects on the basis of their (structured) value, and as such is based on exact match queries (extended with the semantics provided by the *is-a* hierarchy).

CORE. (COntent-based Retrieval Engine) [40] is an MM system explicitly designed to support content-based queries. CORE provides a model which manages multiple media (mainly audio, video, images and their composition). A multimedia object is represented through a set of features and a set of concepts, identified through an interpretation process. The same object may have multiple features and multiple interpretations. CORE manages the relationships among objects: super and sub object relations as well as generic relations. The retrieval of an MM object relies on a set of feature similarity measures (for matching feature values) and on the concept of *fuzzy* similarity to compare a concept with the interpretations assigned to MM objects through their feature values. Complex queries are dealt with by combining with a weighted sum the contribution of the single query terms (which can be attribute values, feature values, and concepts).

SCORE. The System for Content based REtrieval (SCORE) is an interesting system specifically designed for retrieving pictures [1]. In SCORE, the contents of a picture consist of a collection of entities, and an ad-hoc Entity-Relationship model is used for associating an entity with its properties and its relationships. The relationships are limited to those that can be directly extracted from the picture containing the entities, this means that action relationships and spatial relationships are directly supported by SCORE model. In this way, a knowledge base with a complete set of rules for deducing complex spatial relationships is used. A visual query interface, which enables text and icons to be combined and that can make use of a notion of relevant feedback, is used to formulate the similarity query. SCORE allows fuzzy matching of attribute values, imprecise matching of non-spatial relationships, and a controlled deduction process of spatial relationships.

Marcus and Subrahmanian. In [29] a logic framework is described. Their approach allows heterogeneous media types to be integrated by introducing the so-called "media instances". The purpose of a media instance is to abstract away specific physical aspects of media data and to provide a "glue" to integrate them into a common environment. What we call "conceptual objects" are referred to as "features" in [29], and are directly attached to MM objects (called "states" in [29]). Content-based retrieval is thus almost reduced to keyword-based search. Since a partial order relationship is defined on the set of "features", to capture the notion of "subfeatures" (e.g., in a Car DB, odometer is a subfeature of dashboard), it is possible to *relax* a query when no match for a given "feature" is found.

Infoscopes. The work done by R. Jain and colleagues (see, e.g., [24, 26]) aims to develop *infoscopes*, which are the information systems of the future [26]. Infoscopes will manage a MM (image) database and a feature database, and will include four basic modules: an interactive query module, an insertion module, a data processing module, and a knowledge module. The latter is used to provide domain-specific information and to support semantic queries. The VIMSYS data model [24, 26] uses several levels of abstraction to support the activities of infoscopes. The lower image representation level is where raw data is stored. Image objects, extracted from image data, constitute the next layer. The two domain-dependent levels of the domain objects and the domain events are built on top of this.

Our model owes some ideas to the approach taken in CORE and VIMSYS. In fact, it is based on the representation of multimedia objects through features and concepts. The retrieval is based on a similarity matching between the query and the retrieved objects. The approach adopted in CORE and VIMSYS has been extended as follows:

1. The model is Object-Oriented: this makes it possible to use O-O support for the representation of the content of multimedia data and the integration of information not directly contained in the multimedia data.

2. The model takes into account the *structure* of multimedia data. This means that the composition of multimedia objects in terms of other objects can be explicitly represented, and that restrictions on the structure of multimedia objects can be expressed in queries.

3. Features and their characteristics are not predefined. New features can be created according to the application needs; existing features can be customized by defining specific extraction functions and functions for measuring the similarity of the values of the features.

4. The interpretation, i.e., the recognition of the concepts in a multimedia object, can be done either while the object is being inserted or when queries involving a specific concept are issued. This approach has two advantages: it enables one to extend the concepts used for classification (for example some concepts can be used only for a specific application); on the other hand it makes it possible to adopt optimization techniques that take into account the tradeoff between flexibility, query execution, and space used for access structures.

5. The Query Language is an extension of a traditional query language. It has been extended to allow the formulation of queries that can simultaneously consider restrictions on features, concepts, and the structural aspects of MMDS objects. Furthermore, the language supports the formulation of queries with imprecise conditions. The outcome of an interrogation is an ordered set of pairs composed of an object together with a degree of matching with respect to the formulated query.

3. An overview of the approach

3.1. Structuring the data model

The Multimedia Data Model is composed of three data models: the Multimedia Description Model (MDM), which allows one to identify relevant position of multimedia data; the Multimedia Presentation Model (MPM), which specifies how MDM objects have to be delivered respecting their temporal and spatial relationships; and the Multimedia Interpretation Model (MIM), which allows the semantic interpretation of multimedia objects to be specified.

At the lowest level of representation, a *multimedia data* is any unstructured piece of information stored in the multimedia database. It can be acquired either from real world interfaces or from other existing multimedia databases. For example, a video sequence can be acquired through a video camera, an image can be digitized through a scanner, and so on. These are the "real" pieces of multimedia data; hereafter we will call them *raw objects* (RO). Examples of ROs are: a Text, a Video, a Raster Image, a Graphical Image, an Audio/Video. None of these data contain any specification regarding internal content and internal structure. A portion of the data contains information about their physical encoding and the remaining data consist of an unstructured linear stream of bytes.

One of the aims of interpreting a set of persistent multimedia data is to make explicit the structure and content present in the multimedia data in order to support their retrieval. The

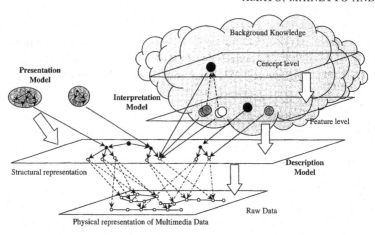

Figure 1. Relationships among the models of an MMDS

interpretation uses abstraction mechanisms and relationships which are both generic, that is independent of modeling needs of multimedia data, and specific for multimedia data. To express queries based on the content of objects, the *Multimedia Interpretation Model* should allow the representation of the semantic content of multimedia objects. The content is represented at two levels: the physical content is described by extracting features from multimedia streams, while a semantic description is obtained by associating object features to predefined concepts. The *Presentation Model* allows complex spatial and temporal relationships to be defined among description level objects in order to create multimedia presentations.

The objects which are interpreted and presented are individuated by using the mechanisms of the *Multimedia Description Model*. It allows one to specify the structure and the composition of all objects that the MMDS manages. In the Multimedia Description Model, the unstructured content of an RO can be conveniently structured by representing portions of it as *basic objects*, and then assembling such basic objects into a *complex object*. Objects of the Multimedia Description Model are those that can be retrieved, manipulated, and delivered. The values of features, which are defined and used in the MIM, are calculated for the objects of the description model, and queries are performed by using these features and their semantic description as arguments. Figure 1 shows how the model is organized.

The rest of the paper will concentrate on retrieval by content in an MMDS. The aspects related to the presentation are not discussed, though the model has been designed to take them into account (through the MPM). For details, see [28, 21, 22].

3.2. A pragmatic view of the MMDS

A block diagram of the analysis and retrieval processes is sketched in Figure 2. We identified three main phases: *database population*, which allows one to insert multimedia data and to extract information about their content; *access structure generation*, which supplies an efficient retrieval of multimedia objects, and *query formulation and execution*.

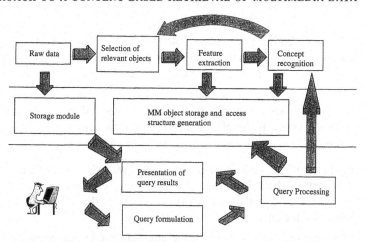

Figure 2. Block diagram of analysis and retrieval processes

Database population. Multimedia data arrive as raw data with (almost) no information about their content, apart from the type of data (e.g., image, video, audio, etc.), the data format (e.g., JPEG, MPEG, TIFF, etc.), and possibly generic information about their content (such as a textual caption or a set of keywords). The raw object is stored as it is in the multimedia database. Its content is analyzed through the following steps:

1. identification of *relevant objects*; a relevant object is any subpart of the multimedia data that contains useful information for retrieving the raw object (note that the entire raw object too can be considered as a relevant object). Relevant objects can be identified by interacting with the user. A relevant object can be related to the concept that is being recognized.

2. Extraction of *features* from relevant objects.

3. Recognition of *concepts* associated with relevant objects. Features are used to determine which concepts apply to the relevant object.

Concepts associated with objects of the description model can be recognized either during the database population or at retrieval time. The first solution requires a pre-analysis when a new multimedia document is inserted into the database. This pre-analysis, which can either be guided by a human expert or completely automatic using recognition methods, tries to discover which concepts are present in the inserted document. The pre-analysis phase determines the *recognition degree* of each concept recognized. Each interpreted relevant object is inserted, together with its recognition degree, into the set associated with the concept.

The second approach does not use pre-analysis. It evaluates at run time the recognition methods associated with the specified concepts. The recognition method can be tuned by users with parameters that allow them to prompt the system to retrieve objects that satisfy their personal idea of the concept being searched for.

The first approach has the drawback of slowing down the insertion of new documents into the database, especially when many concepts are present in the database. Furthermore, since concept identification is often subjective, the resulting set is always obtained through the personal suggestions of the person who tuned the analyzer when the system was set-up. However, this approach does allow fast evaluations of conceptual level queries.

The second approach allows faster insertion of new elements since it only requires the feature extraction process. It also allows users to tune their search to get more relevant results. However, it leads to a slower execution of conceptual level queries.

Access structure generation. Using feature and concept values the system creates appropriate access structures that will speedup the subsequent retrieval process. The access structures must be able to support similarity retrieval, i.e., the retrieval of all objects which are *similar* to the query.

Several access structures have been studied to this end; their characteristics depend on the characteristics of the space where the feature values are placed. If the space is a *vector space*, i.e., feature values are represented through vectors in an n-dimensional space, the most commonly used access structures are *Grid files* [30], R-tree and its variations [25, 5, 38], TV-tree [27]. If the space is metric (i.e., there exists a distance metric which satisfies the triangle inequality) but it is not a vector space, data partitioning can be based only on the distance function between the objects stored; access structures for this type of data include those reported in [13, 7, 14]. The most general class is that of spaces which are not metric; an access structure that can be used for this purpose includes the signature files [18] and its variations to support partial match retrieval [15] and to provide support for content based retrieval of images [36, 35].

Query formulation and execution. The user formulates the *query* by interacting with the graphical interface provided by the *Query Formulation Tool*. Various forms of query formulation can be supported [26]. The *Query Formulation Tool* also has the task of transforming the query into a *symbolic query*, which is processed by the *Query Processor* of the MMDS. The *Query Processor* evaluates the *symbolic query*, giving as an outcome a set of objects with an associated *matching degree* which measures the *similarity* between the query and the retrieved object. The *Query Results Presentation Tool* presents the results in decreasing order of relevance. The *Query Optimiser* component of the *Query Processor* can use the access data structures built during database population, and it can request that new concepts are recognized at query time.

According to [26], the *Query Formulation Tool* allows the following types of queries to be expressed:

Symbolic Queries. Users have quite a precise knowledge both of what they are looking for and the information associated with the multimedia objects in the database. To express these queries the user may directly use an SQL-like query language.

Query by Example. An object of the database (or part of an object) is used to formulate the query, asking for all objects which are similar to the given object. Using tools for the manipulation of multimedia data, the user may also modify the multimedia object, by taking only parts of an object, by composing different objects, or by modifying parts of an object (e.g., a color, a texture, the shape, etc.).

4. A model for content based retrieval of Multimedia Data

This section highlights the aspects of the model that are interesting for performing content-based retrieval of multimedia data. For completeness, we first present the physical organization of multimedia data. The paper then illustrates the core part of our MMDS, i.e., description and interpretation models.

In this section we will sometimes try to be precise without being very formal by using the well-known operators used in semantic domain construction such as: function ($\rightarrow$), cartesian product ($\times$), union ($+$), and repetition ($*$).

4.1. Storing and Accessing Multimedia Data: the Physical Level

The physical level does not have any knowledge about the content of multimedia data. The operations of the physical level are not aware of the internal logical organization of a multimedia datum, and, for performance reasons, they are mainly interested in the way in which multimedia data are stored and accessed. This aspect, which is outside the scope of this paper, includes issues such as data placement for continuous media, data striping and data interleaving, management of tertiary storage and storage hierarchies, etc. [20].

At the physical level, from the retrieval point of view, multimedia data are simply viewed as long unstructured sequences of bytes, that is as *raw objects* (ROs). Each RO has an *object identity* and its *state* is an unstructured sequence of bytes.

A multimedia database can contain several different kinds of ROs: Text, Audio, Video, Raster Image, Graphical Image, and Audio/Video. Each RO is represented by a triple **(ROBJ, Obj-attributes, Obj-default-constraints)** where:

- **ROBJ** is the physical object identifier that uniquely identifies the RO.

- **Obj-attributes** is a set of attributes that specify the characteristics of the RO. These attributes are media dependent. For example, in a video object these attributes can specify the coding format (e.g., MPEG-1 video), the duration, the creation date and time, etc.

- **Obj-default-constraints** are a set of parameters that specify constraints for obtaining a presentation of the highest quality. For example, in a video object the Obj-default-constraints could specify that the actual frame rate for playing the video is 20 frames/sec, that the resolution is 640x480 and so on.

The interface of the physical level is made up of primitives that are useful for inserting multimedia data into the database, for retrieving, and for editing existing documents in the database:

- *creation* of an empty RO, i.e., an RO with an identity and a state represented by an empty sequence of bytes;

- *appendage* to the state of an existing RO of a byte sequence.

- *deletion* of an RO with a given identity,

- *access* to the whole sequence of bytes associated with an RO of a given identity,

- *access* to a subsequence of the sequence and

- *removal* of a subsequence with compactation of the remaining long sequence of bytes.

Note that these operations allow higher level operations to be implemented that can adopt non-destructive editing techniques for dealing with ROs.

4.2. The Multimedia Description Model

A raw object contains a large amount of significant information that cannot easily be managed unless its structure is explicitly represented. The description model serves this purpose. It provides the linguistic mechanisms for defining and manipulating a structured representation of the information contained in raw objects.

The Multimedia Description Model must provide the linguistic mechanism for identifying the huge amount of conceptual entities stored in ROs. We think the object-oriented data model is the best for this task, especially because it is the closest to the organization of real world entities [2]. The most attractive feature of the object-oriented data model is that there is a one-to-one correspondence between real world entities and entities of the model. This means that every real world entity can be represented by exactly one object. We want to define an object-oriented data model that allows a portion of a long sequence of bytes to be managed as an object on its own.

The basic components of the description model are *canonical media* objects and *media objects*. Both canonical and media objects are similar to basic values such as integers, reals, characters, and so on. A canonical media object is a higher level view of a raw object and corresponds to the entire raw object. A media object represents a relevant portion of a canonical media object.

For every RO in the database a *canonical media object* (CO) is generated at the description level. When it is necessary to *identify* relevant portions of a canonical media object *media objects* (MO) are used. This happens, for example, during the classification of COs: some portions of the object are analyzed in order to recognize the presence of a specific concept. Examples of MOs are regions of images, sequences of regions of video frames, video shots, video episodes, and words or paragraphs in text documents.

The process of identifying an MO depends on the interpretation of COs, and, more in general, on the computational requirements of applications supported by the MMDS. Figure 3 gives a graphical representation of the application of identification to a text RO.

A CO is identified by its *unique identifier*. Each CO identifier is associated with the identifier of the RO it represents and with the set of MOs that refers portions of this CO. The specification of a canonical media object is:

CO   = *Identifiers of canonical media objects*
MCO   = CO → CMOSTAT   Identifiers associated with states
CMOSTAT = ROBJ × MO*   Canonical media object state

An MO has a *unique identifier*, a *state* and a *descriptor (desc)*. The *state* is a pair *(o,desc)*, which indicates that the MO is the subpart of the object *o* individuated by the finite set of

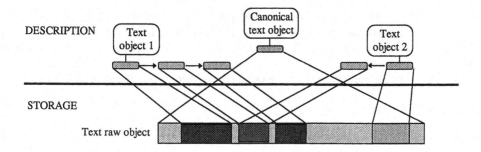

Figure 3. Raw, canonical and media objects

regions encoded in *desc*. Object *o* can be a canonical object (CO) as well as a media objec (MO). The encoding *desc* depends on the type of the raw datum. For instance, in the cas of plain text the encoding can be a sequence of intervals, each represented as a pair c initial and final positions in the raw stream. The encoding can be expressed via a set c intervals for bit-mapped images without compression. Usually more complex multimedi data types require more complex encoding of intervals. For example, arbitrarily shape video sequences can be encoded by using the method proposed by Chang and Messerschmi [12].

Here is the specification of a media object:

MO   = *Identifier of media objects*
MMO   = MO → MOSTAT   Identifiers and associated states
MOSTAT   = (CO + MO) × DESC   Media object state
DESC   = *Encoding of a finite set of regions in the referred media object*

The description model supports the *aggregation* of MOs into *complex objects* in orde to model arbitrarily complex entities and the grouping of objects into *classes*. This ca be obtained through the integration of MOs and COs into an existing object-oriented dat model, as follows:

CXO   = *Identifiers of complex objects*
DCLASS   = *Identifiers of OO classes*
DO   = MO + CO + CXO   Identifiers of Description Objs
MDCLASS = DCLASS → (DO* × FID*)   Description classes

CO denotes the identifier of complex objects while DCLASS is the identifier of the classes The objects of the description model are canonical objects, media objects and traditional OC objects. Classes are associated with extents which are pairs of description model object: and feature identifiers, i.e., *(do*, fid*)*.

Note that all MOs, including canonical objects, have different identities, even those tha insist on the same canonical object. In the most general case, an MO represents a sorted se of byte sub-sequences of a raw object. For example, suppose that an application needs tc isolate the audio stream of a PAL audio/video raw object, where the audio and video data are interleaved into a single BLOB with audio samples following the associated video frame

In this case, the whole audio stream will consist of the sorted set of all audio samples that are present in the original PAL video. This example highlights that sometimes the process of identification can isolate an MO with a different type from the type of the canonical object it derives from.

The operations defined on MOs are the usual editing primitives. They include:

- *creation* of a new MO;

- *modification* of a single an MO;

- *access* to the complete value of an MO;

- *removal* of an entire MO.

- *compact*, which allows one to reorganize the storage for all MOs that share the same raw data.

These operations are usually implemented by means of non-destructive editing techniques that manage a table organized like a B-tree (see for example EXODUS [9]).

Since several MOs can share the same multimedia data, implicit integrity constraints are defined in the Description Model. These integrity constraints resemble those usually defined for composite objects in some OO data model like ORION [4]. They enforce the following two sequences of events to take place: a new MO can only be created after the creation of the referred CO or MO; when a CO or an MO is deleted, all MOs that share it are deleted too (or, on the contrary, the MMDS automatically rejects the deletion of the MO or CO).

4.3. *The Multimedia Interpretation Model*

Two levels of representation are considered in the interpretation model: the *feature level* and the *concept level*. The feature level manages recognizable measurable aspects of description level objects. Color distributions, shapes and textures are, for instance, typically managed at the feature level. The concept level describes the semantic content of the description level objects. At the concept level things such as which conceptual entities are contained in an object and which relations hold among entities are described.

At the feature level each description level object is indexed using its features. Description level objects can be retrieved by submitting similarity queries on features. At the concept level each relevant concept is mapped into the description level objects that match the concept.

4.3.1. Feature level   Description level objects contain several properties that can be measured starting from their physical representation. We call a *feature* a specific kind of measure that can be taken on a multimedia document, and a *feature value* a specific value resulting from measuring some feature in a multimedia document.

A feature is mainly characterised by a *feature extraction function* and by a *similarity function*. A feature extraction function extracts and materializes useful intrinsic properties of an MO. The features can regard both the content of an MO in its entirety and a specific part of its content. Color distributions, shapes, textures, color of eyes, color of hair, position and motion vectors are the examples of features that can be extracted from a graphical MO. The feature *position* may be associated with methods to measure the relative position of two (or more) objects: for example, an operation such as *left_to(O_1, O_2)* returns *true* or *false* depending on the relative position of O_1 and O_2. When a feature value for a certain feature is extracted from a description level object, the object can be indexed using the feature value as an index entry, and can be retrieved using a similarity query on features. The similarity function should be used to compare two different feature values of the same feature. It returns a grade of similarity in the range [0,1]. With the use of features, users can submit queries that refer physical attributes of multimedia documents. For instance queries such as "give me all objects whose dominant color is red, that are moving toward left starting near the upper left corner of the screen" can be asked provided that dominant color extraction, spatial analysis and motion analysis are performed.

A feature is a quintuple *(fid, dclass, extrf, simf, ftype)*:

- The identifier *fid* identifies a feature and corresponds to the feature's name. Color, texture, hair length, eye color, and shape are examples of features.

- *dclass* is a class of objects at the description level. The feature *fid* can be extracted from objects belonging to *dclass*. For example, we extract features from the class "Images" that are different from those extracted from objects of the class "Videos".

- The extraction function *extrf* is the algorithm that extracts feature values from a description level object. Intelligent algorithms are often required to perform this task, since features cannot always be measured easily.

- The similarity function *simf* measures the similarity between two feature values and it returns a value in the interval [0,1]. This function is used during the execution of queries, in order to measure the similarity between a feature value in the query and a feature value of objects to be retrieved.

- *ftype* is used for representing feature values. A feature may have a value which is more complex than a simple integer or real; for example, a histogram of color distribution, or a feature which represents the shape of an object.

A formal definition of features is the following:

FEATURE = (FID × DCLASS × EXTRF × SIMF × FTYPE)		Features
FID	= *Identifier*	Feature identifier
EXTRF	= DO → FTYPE	Feature extractor
SIMF	= (FTYPE × FTYPE) → [0,1]	Similarity function
FTYPE	= *Arbitrarily complex value*	Feature value type

In the previous definition we have to enforce the constraint that FID × DCLASS is unique. The particular difficulties of extracting features in multimedia data environments can mainly be attributed to the following properties:

- features are subjective, thus multiple interpretations are needed; even a specific application may entail dealing with data with different perceptions;

- features are difficult to describe and their identification often requires advanced and time-consuming extraction techniques;

- features typically represent only abstractions (or approximations) of real entities;

- similarity queries are typical due to the imprecision in features and uncertainty in query specification.

Interpretation of features on the concept-level is usually even more difficult because:

- interpretations are application and domain dependent;

- specific interpretation models, often based on sophisticated AI techniques, are applied;

- strict performance constraints are typically required that ask for efficient implementation techniques to be applied.

Features are not only used to support query by content, but they are also used to map concepts and objects at the description level. This characteristic is discussed in detail in the next subsection.

4.3.2. Conceptual level   The conceptual data model provides an object oriented classification of description level objects. This is obtained by using a mapping mechanism that expresses the correspondence between conceptual level aspects and description level aspects.

The conceptual class *Person*, for instance, besides containing conceptual objects representing information on persons, that is its instances, may also be used to represent all description level objects that contain persons. For example, the instance "Bill Clinton" of the class *Person*, may also represent the description level objects that contain Bill Clinton.

Concepts can be mapped into description level objects using two approaches. The first approach, which we call *static mapping*, uses some static references that link each concept with the description level objects that contain it. Static references can be generated when a new document is inserted into the database by an automatic classifier or by the user who is inserting the object. The second approach, called *dynamic mapping*, evaluates at run-time a tunable function, called the *membership function*, in order to match the concept. The membership function may refer features and other known concepts as well.

The static mapping increases the time needed to insert new objects into the database, above all if several concepts are considered, but allows faster evaluations of conceptual level queries.

The dynamic mapping enables faster insertion of new elements since it requires only the extraction of feature values. Furthermore, concept recognition can be tuned at search time in order to improve the quality of retrieval. The drawback is in terms of performance during the execution of conceptual level queries.

The choice of the optimal strategy to map concepts into description level objects is left to the database administrator. At query time users may use one of the two strategies, according to the type of optimization they prefer: efficiency or effectiveness.

The concept model also behaves like a classical object data model so it even allows information to be represented that is not explicitly contained in multimedia documents. The information contained in a multimedia document is only a partial representation of the information present in the real world. For instance, the name of a person or his date of birth cannot be inferred from a picture. This kind of information represents the *background knowledge* and can be described at the conceptual level by adding the missing information to concepts. Relationships among concepts can be described at this level; for example, the concept *skyscraper* is a specialization of the concept *building*. The relationships among concepts can be used for query relaxation allowing one concept to be substituted with another in the query.

Below is a formal description of a concept level object, of a concept level class, and of the mapping between concepts and description level objects:

Objects. An object has a unique identifier. The identifier is mapped into the object state represented by a triple *(stat, smap, dmap)* where

- *stat* is the traditional state of an object, i.e., the record that represents it and its methods,
- *smap* represents support for static mapping,
- *dmap* represents support for dynamic mapping.

A conceptual object can be mapped into objects belonging to different description level classes. This is done by associating each object with a set of static and dynamic mapping. Each element of the set is specialized for a specific description level class.

Static mapping is obtained by using a set of pairs *(dclass, rlist)* where

- *dclass* is a class of the description level. The conceptual object is mapped into objects of *dclass*.
- *rlist* is a ranked list of objects of *dclass*. A ranked list is needed since concept recognition may be uncertain.

The dynamic mapping is obtained by associating each object with a set of pairs *(dclass, mf)* where

- *dclass* is a class of the description level. The conceptual object is mapped into objects of *dclass*.
- *mf* is the membership function that determines the degree of matching between objects belonging to *dclass* and the concept.

A formal specification of the concept level objects is:

OBJ	= *Identifier*	Concept level objects
MOBJ	= OBJ → OSTAT	Identifier mapped into states
OSTAT	= (STAT × SMAP × DMAP)	Object state
SMAP	= (DCLASS × RTLIST)*	Static mapping
DMAP	= (DCLASS × MF)*	Dynamic mapping
RLIST	= (DO × RD)*	Ranked list
STAT	= REC × METHODS	Classical state

Classes. Each class has an extent that contains objects of the concept level, and some mechanisms that provide the conceptual interpretation of objects of the description level.

A class has an identifier that is mapped into a pair (*extent, dmap*) where

- *extent* is the sequence of objects that are instances of the class
- *dmap* is the support for dynamic mapping.

The mapping of a class into description level objects can either be obtained by directly using its mapping methods, or by mapping each of its instances contained in the extent. Subclasses and instances of classes inherit mapping methods from super-classes and from the class they belong to respectively. A mapping method can be refined and overwritten in subclasses and instances of classes.

A formal specification for classes is:

CLASS	= *Identifier*	Class Identifier
MCLASS	= CLASS → (EXTENT × DMAP)	Class map
EXTENT	= OBJ*	Extent

Membership function. A membership function is used to evaluate the degree of recognition of a concept for an object of the description level. Its formal specification is:

$$MF = (DO × PAR) → RD$$

This states that the membership function has as input parameters an object of the description level plus parameters that can be used to modify the behavior of the function. The output is the recognition degree of the conceptual object (which is a grade that measures how well the object matches the concept).

Various strategies can be used to implement a membership function. We have identified three types of strategies:

- An object of the description level (*dobj*) can be classified by using a prototype of the concept. This prototype is either compared with the features extracted from (*dobj*) in order to measure the degree of matching or the correspondence is performed by the user (this corresponds to manual classification).

- The concept is recognized in the description level object by using some feature values. The degree of recognition of the concept is obtained by comparing these feature values with those extracted from the object of the description level to be classified.

- The concept is recognized in the description level object because other concepts have already been recognized.

Let us consider the *tire* concept. Let us suppose that *dobj* is an object of the description level. The *color* and *shape* features are extracted from *dobj*. Let us suppose that $extrf_{shape}(dobj) = ellipse$ and $extrf_{color}(dobj) = brown$. The membership function of the *tire* concept requires the presence of an object with a *shape* feature that has the value *circle* and with a *color* that has the value *black*. The membership function measures the degree of recognition of the concept *tire* in the object *dobj* through the similarity of the values of features *color* and *shape* in *dobj*, and the values *circle* and *black* indicated in the membership function.

As a more complex example, let us consider the *car* concept. We assume that it can be recognized by searching for some particular shape and some relevant object, corresponding to the *tire* concept, positioned in some particular position. The *Ferrari testarossa* object, belonging to the car conceptual class, can be recognized using the membership function of the car class and adding a specific description that allows it to be distinguish from the other cars.

5. Querying the Multimedia Database

There are basically two modes for visiting a multimedia database:

browsing, where users have foggy ideas of what they are looking for and are interested in sample objects which might be used for retrieval;

content-based retrieval, where a request is specified and (a relevance-based) retrieval of objects satisfying the query is expected.

Content-based retrieval in multimedia environments generally takes the form of *similarity queries* [40, 33, 34, 8, 16, 17]. Similarity queries are needed when:

- an exact comparison is not possible, it is either too restrictive or it may even lead to empty results; the data is vague and/or the user is not able to make precise queries;

- retrieved objects need to be ranked so that the set of retrieved objects can be restricted and/or qualifying objects shown to the user in decreasing order of relevance.

A query may contain the following types of restrictions:

Features and Concepts The user may express restrictions on the values of the *object's features* or on the values of *concepts*. Both types of restrictions can be expressed either as a *symbolic query* or through the *query by example* mechanism. Queries on *concept* values are usually *domain dependent*.

Object Structure. Single media objects as well as multimedia objects are structured, as illustrated in the previous section. The *query formulation tool* will allow the user to make restrictions on the structure of the multimedia objects to be retrieved.

Spatio-temporal Relationships. An important characteristic of multimedia data is related to the spatial and temporal relationships among different objects. The user should have the possibility to formulate restrictions on the spatial and temporal relationships of the objects to be retrieved. Again, the query can be formulated through a *symbolic query language* or through a *query by example* procedure.

This kind of query restriction can be expressed in our model if specific features for object spatial and temporal position have been defined. These features also entail defining operations to measure the relative position of two (or more) objects.

Uncertainty. The *query formulation tool* will allow users to express their uncertainty regarding some of the restrictions formulated and their preferences for some conditions. For example, users may not be certain of the color of an object, while they are sure about the presence of an object. The values of preference and uncertainty will be used to measure the degree of matching between the query and the retrieved objects.

5.1.   The MM Query Language

This section outlines the *Multimedia Symbolic Query Language (MMSQL)*. We will focus on the basic constructs that the query language provides.

The MMSQL has the standard functionalities of an O-O query language (such as, for example OQL [10]) extended in order to deal with imprecise information and uncertain interpretations of multimedia objects. This leads to a modification of the set operations *union, intersection, difference* and *cartesian product* and to the adoption of operators to test the *similarity* between feature values and the *partial match* between a concept and the interpretation of a description object. The evaluation of a query returns a *ranked set* of objects. Each element in the set has an associated value that provides a measure of the degree of match with the query. We are not going to describe how queries are executed; however, the data model described in previous sections and the query language we are going to describe, are able to support the management of query relaxation. This means that if the user specified a certain concept in the query, the answer set may also contain objects that do not contain that concept but other related concepts (defined through a relationship between concepts).

A query has the typical `select-from-where` structure:

```
Q = select <select-list>
    from   <from-list>
    where  <condition>
```

where

- `<from-list>` is the root of the query. It specifies the set of objects that are candidates to be returned by the query.

  The root of a query can be one of the following elements: a *conceptual class*, a *description level class*, a *query*, the *union* **U**, *intersection* **I**, *difference* **D** or *Cartesian product* **X** of two queries:

  $$\begin{aligned}
  \text{<from-list>} = \ &\text{CLASS} \mid \\
  &\text{DCLASS} \mid \\
  &Q \mid \\
  &\mathbf{U}(Q_1, w_1, Q_2, w_2) \mid \\
  &\mathbf{I}(Q_1, w_1, Q_2, w_2) \mid \\
  &\mathbf{D}(Q_1, w_1, Q_2, w_2) \mid \\
  &\mathbf{X}(Q_1, w_1, Q_2, w_2)
  \end{aligned}$$

  Union, intersection, difference and cartesian product are all operations that do not follow the *boolean logic*. For example, $\mathbf{U}(Q_1, w_1, Q_2, w_2)$ represents the union of queries Q_1 and Q_2 with a relative importance w_1 and w_2 respectively. This operation will perform the union of the results of Q_1 and Q_2; the degree of matching of each object will depend on its degree of matching in Q_1 (resp. Q_2) and the relative importance w_1 (resp. w_2).

- `<select-list>` is an expression that specifies what a query should return for each element of the from-list that has been validated in the query condition. It represents the projection of the query. The query projection is a valid expression based on constants and on paths rooted at `<from-list>`.

  For example, if the from-list of the query contains the *class Persons* with an attribute *Name*, then a valid expression for the select-list would be *Persons.Name*.

- `<condition>` is the query condition. It can be a simple condition or a complex condition; complex conditions are composed of simple and complex conditions. A simple condition is composed of precise and imprecise comparisons:

  $$\begin{aligned}
  \text{<condition>} = \ &\text{<simple-condition>} \mid \\
  &\text{<complex-condition>}
  \end{aligned}$$

  $$\begin{aligned}
  \text{<simple-condition>} = \ &\text{<precise-comparison>} \mid \\
  &\text{<imprecise-comparison>}
  \end{aligned}$$

The `<condition>` is an expression e; the evaluation of e for an object individuated by the `<from-list>` returns its recognition degree (hereafter expressed as e). The `<precise-comparison>` is an expression that contains the usual comparison expressions such as equal, less-than, and greater-than.

Below we describe the `<imprecise-comparison>` expressions. v indicates expressions that return a generic value, o expressions that return a generic object, do expressions that return an object of the description level, mo expressions that return a media object, c expressions that return a concept, w weights to be associated with to expressions for the imprecise comparisons, and fv expressions that return feature values.

Imprecise comparison. Imprecise comparison operators are needed when feature values are compared, when concepts are mapped into description level objects, and when ranked set operations are performed. An imprecise comparison is composed of the following constructs:

fv_1 sim fv_2	similarities between feature values
do match c	tests whether a description object matches a concept
v in Q	tests whether a value belongs to a ranked set

The *sim* operator is used to evaluate the similarity between two feature values. It is calculated by using the similarity function defined for the feature. The *match* operator measures the degree of matching of a concept c in a description object do. The *in* operator tests whether a value belongs to a ranked set. This operation returns the recognition degree of the tested element.

Complex conditions. Simple conditions can be combined into complex conditions through the use of *and, or* and *not* operators. In the following we consider that two expressions, e_1 and e_2 have to be combined. Expression e_1 (resp. e_2) has a relevance w_1 (w_2). The relevance allows one to specify the weight to be assigned to each expression. It takes into account the uncertainty that users may have regarding some of the conditions they are expressing (for example they want to express that it is much more important that the retrieved images contain a church rather than of a bell tower). The proposed operators are the following:

$e_1[, w_1]$ and $e_2[, w_2]$
$e_1[, w_1]$ or $e_2[, w_2]$
not e

The query language does not impose any constraints on the method to be used to compute the recognition degree of the complex expressions. This is a task of the query processor, which is not described in the paper. However, various approaches can be followed, such as the adoption of fuzzy logic, probabilistic logic, or the probabilistic model of Information Retrieval [37].

The language is not tied to a specific approach whose validity has still not been demonstrated. The query language uses constructs that deal with imprecision and it manages recognition degrees, but we do not restrict it to a specific approach. However, a specific approach must be defined when the language is implemented, since its choice affects implementation and optimization techniques.

The intuitive meaning of the *and* and *or* operators should be preserved, irrespective of the implementation: the use of the *and* operator means that both recognition degrees of the terms should be high; the use of the *or* operator means that only one of the recognition degrees should be high. The difference between the actual behavior and the intuitive behavior of the language can be considered as a matter of precision and it is often subjective. Since the information is also intrinsically imprecise, the user may also use the language without knowing the actual implementation of constructs. Users

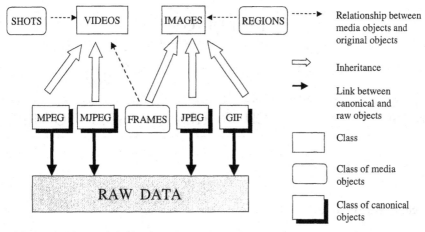

Figure 4. Schema of the description level

may only use their intuitive ideas of the behavior knowing that the results are affected by a certain degree of imprecision.

Selectors. The language will support all traditional expressions of an object oriented query language and new constructs which depend on the model proposed. In particular, specific selectors are needed to cope with features, recognition degrees and structure, in addition to traditional selectors for accessing fields of structured values and for evaluating the methods of objects:

v.attribute	access of an attribute of a structure or of an object
o.method(args)	object method evaluation
*o.*feature*(fid)*	access of features of description level objects
*v.*rank	evaluation of the recognition degree of a value
*mo.*part_of	returns the description object which *mo* was extracted from

Given an object of the description level, it is possible to access its feature value that corresponds to the feature *fid* by using the *feature* selector. This entails accessing the feature values that have already been extracted while objects where being inserted into the database.

The *rank* selector is used to access the recognition degree of a value. Comparison and logical operators modify the recognition degree of the value that is being evaluated.

A media object can be extracted from a canonical object or from another media object. The *part_of* selector applied to a media object, returns the object it has been extracted from.

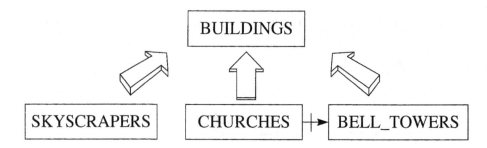

Figure 5. Schema of the conceptual level

6. A complete example

6.1. The schema

Let us consider the description level schema shown in Figure 4. In that schema, four classes contain canonical objects: MPEG for mpeg encoded videos, MJPEG for motion jpeg encoded videos, JPEG for jpeg encoded images, and GIF for gif encoded images. MPEG and MJPEG are subclasses of the VIDEOS class. Media objects for the SHOTS and FRAMES classes are extracted from objects of the VIDEOS class. The classes FRAMES, JPEG and GIF are subclasses of the class IMAGES. Media objects for the REGIONS class are extracted from objects of the class IMAGES. From each object of the class IMAGES we extract the features *color* and *shape*.

The schema for the conceptual level is shown in Figure 5. Let us suppose that at the conceptual level we want to describe important buildings. In particular, we want to store information for skyscrapers, churches and bell towers.

The SKYSCRAPERS, CHURCHES and BELL_TOWERS classes are subclasses of the BUILDINGS class. Objects of the CHURCHES class have the reference bell_tower which indicates their bell tower if they have one. All buildings have the attribute name. All skyscrapers have the attribute height which specifies the height of the skyscraper represented.

Static and dynamic mappings are defined for each object of the classes of the conceptual level. These mappings allow conceptual level objects to be mapped into description level objects. In this example we do not specify how these mappings take place. We just suppose that they have been set, either manually or automatically, when objects and classes have been created. Figure 6 shows an example of an image of the class IMAGES and also a number of relevant parts which have been identified as regions belonging to the class REGIONS. For each of these objects, the features *color* and *shape* have been extracted and a certain number of concepts identified.

6.2. Queries

EXAMPLE: Let us suppose that a user needs to *"retrieve all images of all skyscrapers that are higher than two hundred meters"*.

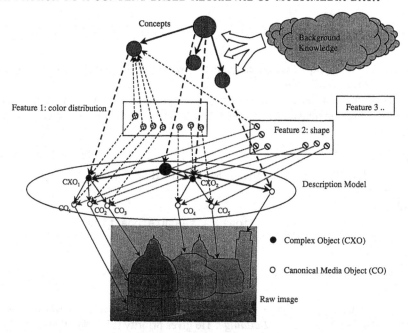

Figure 6. Example of the mappings from raw level, description level and interpretation level

The user can first restrict the objects of the SKYSCRAPERS class whose *height* attribute has a value greater that two hundred. The resulting objects can then be matched with objects of the class IMAGES of the description level.

```
select I
from I in IMAGES
where I match any
        (select SS
         from SS in SKYSCRAPERS
         where SS.height > 200)
```

□

EXAMPLE: Let us suppose that a user wants to *"retrieve all images that contain churches with their bell tower"*. He gives priority to the fact that in the image there is a church instead of the fact that there is a bell tower.

The query performs a cartesian product between the IMAGES and the CHURCHES classes then it only keeps the images that match both the church and its bell tower:

```
select I
from C in CHURCHES, I in IMAGES
where
  (I match C),(0.6)
  and
  (I match C.bell_tower),(0.4)
```

□

EXAMPLE: Let us suppose that a user wants to "*retrieve all images that contain churches with their bell tower on the left*".

The query performs a Cartesian product then it keeps the images with a region matching the church and a region matching the bell tower with the condition that the second is on the left of the first.

```
select I
from C in CHURCHES, I in IMAGES, R1 in REGIONS, R2 in REGIONS
where   R1 match C
  and R2 match C.bell_tower
  and left_to(R2.feature(position),R1.feature(position))
  and R1.part_of = I
  and R2.part_of = I;
```

□

EXAMPLE: Let us suppose that a user wants to "*retrieve all buildings whose shape is similar to that of the Empire State Building*". He gives priority to the fact that a region is a building instead of the fact that it is similar to the Empire State Building.

The query should first retrieve all regions that match the Empire State Building. Then, all regions that match some building and whose shape is similar to that of the regions containing the Empire State Building are retrieved. Since it is more important that a region is a building than that it is similar to the Empire State Building, we use the weight 0.7 for the first clause and 0.3 for the second:

```
select B
from R1 in REGIONS, B in BUILDINGS
where   (R1.feature(SHAPE) sim any
        (select R.feature(SHAPE)
         from R in REGIONS
         where R match
         (select SS
          from SS in SKYSCRAPERS
          where SS.name='Empire State Building'))),(0.3)
        and (R1 match B),(0.7);
```

□

7. Conclusions and future work

In this paper we have presented a Multimedia Data Model that provides support for content-based retrieval of multimedia objects. It also offers the possibility for the integration of a presentation model, and the integration of different implementation approaches and partial modelling efforts. We have also outlined a Query Language that uses the features offered by the model.

The main features of the model are that (i) it is Object-Oriented, which makes it possible to use an object-oriented representation of the content of multimedia data as well as of all information that is not explicitly contained in the multimedia data; (ii) it allows one to represent the *structure* of multimedia objects, making the composition of objects explicit in terms of other objects (for example, Figure 6 shows that the Baptistery in Pisa can be represented as three parts); (iii) the contents of multimedia objects can be represented by taking into account their physical values (*feature values*) as well as their semantic content (*concepts*); (iv) the definition of *features* and *concepts* is not predefined, so that new features and concepts can be created according to the application needs; (v) concepts can be defined through the use of information extracted from the multimedia objects (the feature values) and by using background knowledge.

We have defined the Query Language starting from a traditional query language and extending it to support (i) partial match retrieval, i.e., all objects are retrieved that are similar to the query at least to a certain degree; (ii) expressions of conditions on the values of features, the presence of concepts and the structure of objects; (iii) possibilities to take into account user uncertainty on some parts of the query; (iv) possibilities to take into account the imprecision of the interpretation of the content of the multimedia object.

The result of a query is a ranked set, that is a set of pairs (object, recognition degree). The recognition degree is a measure of the degree of match between the query and the object.

Our future work will evolve in the following directions:

- Research how to combine similarity degrees deriving from different features and concepts.

- Investigate the implications of these models with the storage and access of multimedia objects. In fact, real application environments will require the storage of many trillions of bytes of data, requiring the use of a storage hierarchy consisting of different layers. This implies that data placement is crucial for effective manipulation of the data and for an efficient retrieval.

- Study of an effective and efficient query processing algorithm.

- Completion of the implementation of a system that supports the proposed model.

Acknowledgments

This work has been partly funded by European Union under ESPRIT Long Term Research Project HERMES, No 9141, and by Project MIDA of Committee 7 of Italian National Research Council.

References

1. Y. Alp Aslandogan, C. Thier, C.T. Yu, C. Liu, and K.R. Nair. "Design, Implementation and Evaluation of SCORE (a System for COntent based REtrieval of Pictures)," in Proceedings of the Eleventh International Conference on Data Engineering (IDCE), Taipei, Taiwan, March 6-10 1995, pp. 280-287.

2. M.P. Atkinson, F. Bancilhon, D. DeWitt, K. Dittrich, D. Maier, and S. Zdonik, "The Object-Oriented Database System Manifesto," in Proceedings of the First DOOD International Conference, Japan, 1989, pp. 40-57.

3. J.R. Bach, C. Fuller, A. Gupta, A. Hampapur, B. Horowitz, R. Humphrey, R. Jain, and C-F. Shu, "The Virage image search engine: An open framework for image management," in Proceedings of the SPIE 96, 1996.

4. J. Banerjee, H. Chou, J.F. Garza, W. Kim, D. Woelk, N. Ballou, and H. Kim, "Data Model Issues for Object-Oriented Applications," ACM Transactions on Office Information Systems, 5(1):3–26, 1987.

5. N. Beckmann, H.-P. Kriegel, R. Schneider, and B. Seeger, "The R*-Tree: an Efficient and Robust Access Method for Points and Rectangles," ACM SIGMOD, pp. 322–331, May 1990.

6. P.B. Berra, F. Golshani, R. Mehrotra, and O.R. Liu-Sheng, "Guest editors' introduction: Multimedia Information Systems," IEEE Transactions on Knowledge and Data Engineering, 5(4):545–550, Aug. 1993.

7. S. Brin, "Near Neighbor Search in Large Metric Space," in Proceedings of the 21st VLDB International Conference, Zurich, Switzerland, September 1995, pages 574–584.

8. A.F. Cardenas, I.T. Ieong, R.K. Taira, R. Barker, and C.M. Breant, "The Knowledge-Based Object-Oriented PICQUERY+ Language," IEEE Transactions on Knowledge and Data Engineering, 5(4):644–657, Aug. 1993.

9. M.J. Carey, D.J. DeWitt, K. Dittrich, J.E. Richardson, and E.J. Shekita, Storage Management for Objects in Exodus, pp. 341–369, 1989.

10. R.G.G. Cattel, "The Object Database Standard: ODMG-93, Release 1.2," Norwell, MA, 1996.

11. S-K. Chang and K-S. Fu, "Picture Query Languages for Pictorial Data-Base Ssystems," IEEE Computer, 14(11):23–42, November 1981.

12. S-F. Chang and D.G. Messerschmitt, "Transform Coding of arbitrarily-shaped Image Segments," in Proceedings of the ACM Conference on Multimedia, 1993.

13. T. Chiueh, "Content-Based Image Indexing," in Proceedings of the 20th VLDB International Conference, Santiago, Chile, September 1994, pp. 582–593.

14. P. Ciaccia, F. Rabitti, and P. Zezula, "A data structure for Similarity Search in Multimedia Databases," in Proc. Of the 9th ERCIM Database Research Group Workshop on Multimedia Databases, Darmstadt, 18-19 March 1996. ERCIM.

15. W.B. Croft and P. Savino, "Implementing Ranking Strategies using Text Signatures," ACM Transactions on Office Information Systems, 6(1):42–62, 1988.

16. Y.F. Day, S. Dagtas, M. Iino, A. Khokhar, and A. Ghafoor, "Object-Oriented Conceptual Modeling of Video Data," in Proc. of the 11th Int. Conf. on Data Engineering, Taiwan, 1995, pp. 401–408.

17. N. Dimitrova and F. Golshani, "Rx for Semantic Video Database Retrieval," in Proceedings of the ACM Multimedia '94, 1994.

18. C. Faloutsos, "Access Methods for Text," ACM Computing Surveys, 17(1):49–74, March 1985.

19. M. Flickner, H. Sawhney, W. Niblack, J. Ashley, Q. Huang, B. Dom, M. Gorkani, J. Hafner, D. Lee, D. Petkovic, D. Steele, and P. Yanker, "Query by image and video content: The QBIC system," IEEE Computer, 28(9):23–32, September 1995.

20. D. Gemmel, H. M. Vin, D. D. Kandlur, P. V. Rangan, and L. A. Rowe, "Multimedia Storage Servers: A Tutorial," IEEE Computer, May 1995, pp. 40–49.

21. A. Ghafoor, "Multimedia Database Management: Perspectives and Challenges," in Proc. Advances in Databases, 13th British National Conf. on Databases, volume 5, July 12-14, 1995, pp. 12–23.

22. S. Gibbs, B. Christian, and D. Tsichritzis, "Data Modeling of Time-Based Media," in Proc. Of ACM SIGMOD Conference on Management of Data, Minneapolis, Minnesota USA, 1994, pp. 92–102.

23. V.N. Gudivada and V.V. Raghavan, "Content-based Image Retrieval Systems: Guest Editors' Introduction," IEEE Computer, September 199, pp. 18–22.

24. A. Gupta, T. Weymouth, and R. Jain, "Semantic Queries with Pictures: The VIMSYS Model," Proc. of 17th International Conference on Very Large Data Bases, September 1991, pp. 69–79.

25. A. Guttman, "R-trees: A Dynamic Index Structure for Spatial Searching," in Proceedings of the 1984 ACM SIGMOD International Conference on Management of Data, Boston, MA, June 1984, pp. 47–57.

26. R. Jain, Infoscopes: Multimedia Information Systems, pp. 217–254, 1996.

27. K-I. Lin, H.V. Jagadish, and C. Faloutsos, "The TV-Tree - an Index Structure for High-Dimensional Data," VLDB Journal, 3:517–542, October 1994.

28. T.D.C. Little and A. Ghafoor. "Interval-Based Conceptual Models for Time-Dependent Multimedia Data," IEEE Transactions on Knowledge and Data Engineering, 5(4):551–562, August 1993.

29. S. Marcus and V.S. Subrahmanian, "Foundations of Multimedia Information Systems," Journal of the ACM, 1996.
30. J. Nievergelt, H. Hinterberger, and K.C. Sevcik, "The Grid File: an Adaptable, Symmetric Multikey File Structure," ACM TODS, 9(1):38–71, March 1984.
31. E. Oomoto and K. Tanaka. "OVID: Design and Implementation of a Video-Object Database System," IEEE Transactions on Knowledge and Data Engineering, 5(4):629–643, August 1993.
32. A. Pentland, R.W. Picard, and S. Sclaroff, "Photobook: Content-based Manipulation in Image Databases," International Journal of Computer Vision, Fall 1995.
33. E.G. Petrakis and C. Faloutsos, "Similarity Searching in Large Image Databases," IEEE Transactions on Knowledge and Data Engineering, 1996.
34. E.G. Petrakis and S.C. Orphanoudakis, "Methodology for the Representation, Indexing and Retrieval of Images by Content," Image and Vision Computing, 11(8):504–521, Oct. 1993.
35. F. Rabitti and P. Savino, "Image Query Processing Based on Multi-Level Signatures," in Proceedings of ACM SIGIR '91, International Conference on Research and Development in Information Retrieval, Chicago, Illinois, 13-16 October 1991, pp. 305–314.
36. F. Rabitti and P. Savino, "An Information Retrieval Approach for Image Databases," in Proceedings of 18th VLDB International Conference, Vancouver, Canada, August 1992, pp. 574–584.
37. G. Salton, Automatic Text Processing - the Transformation, Analysis and Retrieval of Information by Computer, Addison-Wesley: Reading, MA, 1989.
38. T.K. Sellis, N. Roussopoulos, and C. Faloutsos, "The R+-tree: A Dynamic Index for Multi-Dimensional Objects," in Proceedings of the 13th VLDB International Conference, Brighton, England, September 1987, pp. 507–518.
39. J.R. Smith and S-F. Chang, "Tools and Techniques for Color Image Retrieval," in Proceedings of the SPIE 96, 1995.
40. J.K. Wu, A.D. Narasimhalu, B.M. Mehtre, C.P. Lam, and Y.J. Gao, "CORE: A Content-based Retrieval Engine for Multimedia Information Systems," Multimedia Systems, 3(1):25–41, Feb. 1995.
41. A. Yoshitaka, S. Kishida, M. Hirakawa, and T. Ichikawa, "Knowledge-assisted Content-Based Retrieval for Multimedia Databases," IEEE Multimedia, pp. 12–20, 1994.

Giuseppe Amato graduated in Computer Science at the University of Pisa, Italy, in 1992. In 1994 he was a member of the research staff at CNR CNUCE in Pisa, working in the area of object-oriented databases and persistent programming languages; since 1995 he has been a member of the research staff at CNR-IEI in Pisa, working in the area of multimedia information systems. He has participated to the CEC funded ESPRIT BRA Project FIDE-2 (Fully Integrated Data Environments) where he has investigated in the areas of object oriented databases and contributed to the design and realisation of the prototype of PIOS (Physically Independent Object Server), an object oriented database server. Currently he is involved in the CEC-funded ESPRIT LTR Project HERMES (Foundations of High Performance Multimedia Information Management Systems), where he is involved in the definition of a model for content based retrieval of multimedia data. He has published scientific papers in many international conferences in the areas of database information systems. His current research interests are multimedia information retrieval, object oriented databases systems, transaction management in object oriented databases and static analysis of database programming languages.

Giovanni Mainetto holds a Laurea in Computer Science, summa cum laude, from the University of Pisa, Italy, 1980. After an initial industrial experience at the research labs of Systems and Management, in 1985 he joined CNUCE-CNR where he is currently a researcher of the Multimedia team. Since then he has been working on Object-Oriented Databases, Persistent and Database Programming Languages, Persistent Object Stores, Static Analysis of Database Programming Languages and, more recently, on Multimedia Databases. He has participated and/or coordinated CNUCE teams involved in several EU/CNR funded research projects in the database area, among which HERMES (Foundations of High Performance Multimedia Information Management Systems), FIDE I-II(Formally Integrated Data Environment), COMANDOS (Construction and Management of Distributed Object Systems), CNR Progetto Finalizzato Sistemi Informatici e Calcolo Parallelo-Sottoprogetto Basi di Dati Evolute. He has been/is member of national and international program/organizational committees of database conferences; he has published scientific papers in international journals and conferences mainly in the area of Database Programming Languages.

Pasquale Savino graduated in Physics at the University of Pisa, Italy, in 1980. From 1983 to 1995 he has worked at the Olivetti Research Labs in Pisa; since 1996 he has been a member of the research staff at CNR-IEI in Pisa, working in the area of multimedia information systems. He has participated and coordinated several CEC-funded research projects in the multimedia area, among which MULTOS (Multimedia Office Systems), OSMOSE (Open Standard for Multimedia Optical Storage Environments), MALIBU (Multimedia And distance Learning In Banking and bUsiness environments), HYTEA (HYperText Authoring), M-CUBE (Multiple Media Multiple Communication Workstation), MIMICS (Multiparty Interactive Multimedia Conferencing Services). Currently he is involved in the CEC-funded ESPRIT LTR Project HERMES (Foundations of High Performance Multimedia Information Management Systems), where he leads the Work Part on Multimedia Content Addressability. He has published scientific papers in many international journals and conferences in the areas of multimedia document retrieval and information retrieval. His current research interests are multimedia information retrieval, multimedia content addressability and indexing.

Multimedia Tools and Applications 7, 37–66 (1998)

Conceptual Modeling and Querying in Multimedia Databases

CHITTA BARAL   chitta@cs.utep.edu
GRACIELA GONZALEZ   chelis@cs.utep.edu
TRAN SON   tson@cs.utep.edu
Department of Computer Science, University of Texas at El Paso, El Paso, Texas 79968, U.S.A.

Abstract. In this paper, we discuss some design principles that will aid in the design and querying of multimedia databases. We use an object-relational data model and argue that multimedia objects should normally have a special attribute called 'core' which stores the real object itself in contrast to the abstraction which is reflected in the rest of the attributes. We present an extension to the ER Diagram that takes advantage of the 'core' notion to facilitate design of multimedia databases. We discuss some desirable features in a query language for multimedia databases: simplifications like the use of path expressions and implicit use of functions (methods) as attributes, and explicit specification of the display layout and format either at the data definition level or query specification level. To materialize this last feature, we propose a display specification extension to SQL (SQL+D) that we have implemented.

Keywords: ER diagram, multimedia database, object relational data model, modeling the WWW

1. Introduction

A Multimedia database (MMDB)[1] differs from a conventional database in that its content may consist of types that are not commonly found in conventional databases. A list of such data includes: pictures (in gif, in jpeg, etc.), sound clips (in au, etc.), movies (in mpeg, in quicktime, etc.), documents (even multimedia documents), applets, and text (in postscript, in dvi, in pdf, etc.).

   With the availability of tremendous amount of digitized multimedia content (from the WWW to the CD-ROMs and video disks) and the increasing affordability of disk space in computers, people and organizations can now consider having multimedia databases. Such databases will make it easier to answer queries or to locate information about multimedia data, without involving physical effort of a person. For example, a multimedia database containing movies and information about them in a virtual video store (i.e., a huge video server) will not only integrate the steps of going to a video store, looking at the (limited) database about movies in the video store, and walking on the aisles looking for a particular movie (which may not be there because of misplacement or because it has not been restacked after it was returned), but also allow us to ask queries about the movies where the query itself has multimedia content. An example would be to give a clip of Joe Pesci in a particular movie and query about movies with 'similar' clips or similar 'dialogue delivery' by Joe Pesci. Many such examples involving images, videos, maps, documents, audio clips, etc. can easily be developed.

In last couple of years the importance of multimedia databases has been recognized. The US Army and University of Maryland Institute of Advanced Computer Studies (UMIACS) organized workshops on multimedia information systems in 1995 (in Washington DC) and 1996 (West point, NY), and plan to organize another one in 1997 in Italy. A special issue of IEEE Computer (September 95, vol. 28, number 9) has been devoted to multimedia databases involving images [8, 16, 18]. But to our knowledge most research in multimedia database design have focussed on a particular kind of multimedia data, and most of them are concerned with what relations are needed to adequately store *the content* of a particular multimedia database (with particular kind of multimedia content). For example, [16] is concerned with images, while [17] is concerned with representing the spatial relationship among objects in pictures, and [15] is concerned with querying the web. Another direction of research on multimedia databases is focused on data structures and algorithms for storing and processing multimedia content [7].

Our goal in this paper is to explore common design principles for multimedia databases in general—not for a particular multimedia database, or for multimedia databases with a particular kind of content. It seems that the time has come to extrapolate, extract and learn the common design principles from particular examples.

1.1. Designing multimedia databases

A multimedia database is different from a multimedia repository;[2] but it is obvious that it is usually built around multimedia repositories.

The question we now need to answer is how to build a multimedia database around a multimedia repository. A partial answer comes from the observation that conventional databases are also built around repositories. For example, the repository behind a supermarket database [20] includes sales receipts, purchase orders, invoices, employment applications, and many other pieces of information.

The observation that both conventional and multimedia databases are built around repositories suggests that many of the techniques and methodologies used in designing conventional databases can be used (with appropriate enhancements and/or modifications) in designing multimedia databases. For example, one of the basis in the conceptual design [3] of a conventional database is the kind of queries that the database is supposed to answer. We should use that same concept when designing a multimedia database around a multimedia repository. Similarly, we would need to consider the relationships among the data elements. An excellent tool that might also be ported over to multimedia database design is the use of an entity-relationship diagram, possibly with extensions to allow for the correct representation of multimedia features. In a later section we describe such extensions in what we call **core entity relationship model** and use it in designing the schema for a multimedia database.

1.2. Data models for multimedia databases

Considering that a multimedia database will either interact with conventional databases or will have a component which is of the conventional kind, we would like to use a data model that is upward compatible with the relational data model—the most widely used data model for conventional databases.

In many content-based approaches to query multimedia data, the content of the multimedia artifacts are abstracted as a relational database and hence normally do not need any new capability.

But, let us consider the following quote:

A picture is worth thousand words.

The implication of the above quote is that, even after we have extracted (manually, semi-automatically and/or automatically) the various features of a picture[3] and stored it in our database, we can never be sure that we have extracted *all*[4] the useful information. There is always a possibility that in the future we may need some additional information (expressed by the picture) which was not extracted from it earlier. Moreover, for some features it may be preferable to extract them during query answering time rather than extracting them before and storing them in a table.

This leads us to the conclusion that we can not just abstract information from a multimedia artifact into a relational database, but rather should have the provision to store the artifacts themselves, and should also be able to specify operations on the artifacts that can be executed at run-time. This requires types that allow multimedia data and the ability to define methods. For example, we should be able to define a relation of the form:

EMPL(name, ssn, position, salary, dept, picture)

where the attribute 'picture' could be of the type "gif-blob", and we should be able to define operations on pictures and possibly other attributes.

SQL3[5] [4, 12] and many of the recent models in object-relational database products such as Illustra [19], Odapter, UniSQL, DB2, Omniscience have this and additional features useful for multimedia databases. Moreover, with the current effort in object-oriented database standards such as ODMG-93 [5] and the ongoing effort on SQL3/OQL merger [1, 22] we can also use object-oriented data models that are upward compatible with the relational model or SQL-89.

2. Modeling MMDB using object relational data models

In this section, we discuss through examples the design and representation of multimedia and semistructured data using object-relational data models. We then identify some salient features common to modeling different multimedia data types. We first start with data description language and then move to the query language.

2.1. Data description language

Example 1.   Consider designing a relational database for movies, where we not only store information about movies but also store the movies themselves. Let us assume that for each movie we have information about its title, year, producer, director, length, filmtype, and prod_studio. This can be easily stored by having a relation called *MOVIE* with attributes as given below.

   MOVIE(Title, Year, Producer, Director, Length, Movie_type, Prod_studio)

But what about the movie itself? Also, what about operators and functions that can be applied to the movie itself? (Such operations might include extracting the opening sequence of the movie, removing all occurrences of the MacDonald arch in the movie, finding similarities between movies, overlaying text or sound in certain sequences of the movie, etc.)

   The current ORDB models offer two approaches.

- *First approach*: We can define a complex type called movie_t, as shown below in the notation of Illustra:

      create type movie_t(
      Title varchar(30),
      Year int,
      Producer varchar(30),
      Director varchar(30),
      Length int,
      Movie_type varchar(30),
      Prod_studio varchar(30),
      MV blob);

      create table movie of type movie_t;

   Now, we can define and register various user-defined operators and functions for the type *movie_t*. The definition of these functions and operators may use the value of the attribute 'MV'.

   One possible[6] drawback of this approach is that we are completely moving away from the relational model and are using the object-oriented model. In the process we are not taking advantage of storing the abstracted attributes (all attributes other than 'MV') of movie in relations.

- *Second approach*: We can add an attribute of an extended type 'movie_blob' to the *Movie* relation. Various user-defined operators and functions will be defined and registered for this extended type.

   Note that one of the main difference between this approach and the first approach is that in the first approach functions and operators are defined for the type movie_t, while in this approach they are defined for the type movie_blob, whose values does not include the abstracted attributes, such as Title, Producer, etc.

   There are two concerns:

   — An intuitive name for this attribute: The most intuitive name perhaps would be to call this attribute 'movie', but that would create confusion with the relation name

'Movie'. Suppose we find another intuitive name for this attribute. Say we call it 'MV'.

— There will always be some confusion between the relation 'Movie' and the object 'Movie.MV'. Since Movie.MV refers to a movie, a user may incorrectly refer to the title of Movie.MV by using the expression Movie.MV.title instead of the correct expression Movie.title.

The confusion arises because of two ways to look at a movie object; the first is the digitized movie itself, and the second is the abstracted information about the movie.

Actually, the confusion between names will also arise in the first approach. For example, for a movie object with object id $m123$, there could be confusion between $m123$ and $m123.MV$.

Based on the above observations, we would like to propose that objects in general and multimedia objects in particular, whether they are represented in the object-oriented style (as in the first approach) or in a relational style (as in the second approach, where the object is a value ADT in the syntax of SQL3), should be allowed to have a special attribute,[7] say called, **'core'**. We propose that this word be a reserved word in the data description language, and used across all objects. By using it across all objects the users would become familiar with it and this would eliminate the confusion discussed earlier. Note that we are not requiring that this should be part of the type definition of all objects. We are saying that if the type definition of an object would like to use an attribute to represent the digitized object itself then it should use a particular name, perhaps 'core', which other objects may also use. Of course the type definition of an 'employee' object may not have this attribute, as we cannot[8] digitize the employee and store it in our database. We hope that the standards committee of SQL3 and ODMG will consider our suggestion.

Example 2. Following our own suggestion we add the special attribute 'Core' to the 'Movie' relation. In this particular example, the attribute 'Core' has the type as 'movie_blob'. After this enhancement, the 'MOVIE' relation becomes

MOVIE(Title, Year, Producer, Director, Length, Movie_type, Prod_studio, Core)

This is the view that the data entry person has about the data. But we allow users who may query the database to have a object-oriented view of the database. For example, the query: "Show the opening sequence of all movies produced by Spielberg in 1993" *should be permitted* to be expressed in a SQL-like language as follows:

SELECT Movie.opening_seq
FROM Movie
WHERE Year = 1993 AND Director = "Spielberg"

Note that the relation, Movie does not have an attribute called opening_seq. It is a function defined on values of type 'movieblob' (which is the type of the attribute Core) and returns values of the same type. This can be described in SQL-3 as follows:

        DECLARE EXTERNAL opening_seq(movie_blob)
                RETURNS movie_blob
        LANGUAGE C;

The meaning of the above is that, the function opening_seq is defined on objects of the type movie_blob and the value of this function is also of the type movie_blob. Also, to obtain the value of the function opening_seq on any object of the type movie_blob, we need to apply the program opening_seq.c to that object.

In summary, since users will be uniformly using the word 'Core' in the data definition language, they are permitted to leave it out in the queries, and the query interpreter is programmed to look at the attribute 'Core' if necessary. In the above example, the query interpreter after failing to find opening_seq defined on the value ADT Movie, knows to look at Movie.Core.

The Movie relation above and other relations that have the special attribute 'Core' will be referred to as core-relations, and we will call the corresponding schema as a *Core-ORDB schema*.

Example 3.   Another example of a core-relation is:

        EMAIL(From, To, Date, Size, Core, Subject)

In this relation all attributes except 'Core' are of standard types. The type of the attribute 'Core' is an extended type and is called 'ascii_email'.

The query, "List the emails of John that contain the word 'tenure' can be expressed in a SQL like language as follows:

        SELECT Email
        FROM Email
        WHERE Email.Keyword["tenure"] = TRUE

The declaration about the function Keyword can be expressed in SQL-3 in the following way:

        DECLARE EXTERNAL Keyword(email_ascii,charstring)
                RETURNS boolean
        LANGUAGE C;

At present we prefer core-relations (because of its relational nature) for modeling multimedia data and in the rest of the paper we will be following the style of the second approach described in Example 1 instead of the first approach. Unlike the data model in Illustra, our core-relations can also be viewed as object classes. This is similar to row-types in SQL-3.

2.2. Query language

In this section, we discuss two aspects that we would like to see in a query language for multimedia databases. One aspect is related to our discussion in the previous section, and the other aspect is related to the SQL3 data model we use. *Both aspects are concerned with making it easier for a user to frame a query.* Since we discussed in the previous section how to simplify queries using 'core', we now discuss the second aspect.

2.2.1. Query simplification using subtable information.   In SQL3, tables are allowed to have subtables. For example, we can specify in SQL3:

CREATE TABLE manager UNDER employee

In Examples 1 and 3 we saw how our use of core-relations makes it easier to express queries. We now give some examples that show how we can take advantage of UNDER relation between tables and take it one step further than SQL3 to simplify queries.

Example 4.   Consider the following schema:

EMPS(ename, salary, dname)
DEPTS(dname, d#, manager)

and the additional information:

MANAGER is a subtable of the table EMPS
DEPTS.manager is of type MANAGER.

Suppose we would like to ask the query: "Find the salary of the manager of department number 23." An intuitive way to express this query in a SQL-like syntax will be the following query which we refer to as Q_A:

SELECT DEPTS.manager.salary
FROM DEPTS
WHERE DEPTS.D# = 23.

In the absence of the subtable information this query is not meaningful, and we would have to think of the attribute 'manager' of the *DEPTS* relation as a simple attribute to store the name of the manager of the department, which would then be used as a way to get the salary in the *EMPS* tuples. The 'regular' version of the above query would be the following query Q_B:

SELECT EMPS.salary
FROM DEPTS, EMPS
WHERE DEPTS.D# = 23 AND EMPS.ename = DEPTS.manager

We will use our data model, particularly the subtable information to present an algorithm that will translate Q_A to Q_B.

To reinforce our point, let us enhance our schema with the additional relation PERS(ssn, name) and subclass information:

EMPS is a subtable of *PERS*.

The query asking to list the social security number of the manager of department number 23 can be expressed in an intuitive manner by the following query Q_C:

SELECT DEPTS.manager.ssn
FROM DEPTS
WHERE DEPTS.D# = 23

In the absence of the subclass information, this query is not meaningful, and again, we would have to make the 'manager' attribute store the manager's name. The meaningful version of it would be the following query Q_D:

SELECT PERS.ssn
FROM DEPTS, PERS
WHERE DEPTS.D# = 23 AND PERS.name = DEPTS.manager

2.2.2. Query simplification: Summary. The two suggestions regarding query simplification in the previous sections: the use of path expressions and the implicit use of functions as attributes, do not exactly follow SQL[9] in two major respects.

• In Example 1 and 3 we have the queries

SELECT Movie.opening_seq()
FROM Movie
WHERE Year = 1993 AND Director = "Spielberg"

SELECT Email
FROM Email
WHERE Email.Keyword("tenure") = TRUE.

where, opening_seq is neither an attribute of the relation Movie, nor it is a function (strictly) defined on elements of Movie. Rather it is a function defined on Movie.Core. Similarly, the function Keyword is a function defined on Email.Core and character strings.
• In Example 4, the queries Q_A and Q_C, needs to be translated to Q_B and Q_D to be meaningful in terms of SQL.

The reason we allow the above two shortcuts is to make it easier for the user to ask a query. For example, in Q_A, the user wants to know the salary of the manager of a particular department. An intuitive path expression that the user can construct without completely knowing the Database schema corresponding to it (the user's needs) is department.manager.salary.

One of the reasons that object-oriented database are attractive is because the data is supposed to be arranged in an intuitive manner[10], which allows the user to ask questions without completely knowing the schema. (This is impossible in a relational database.) We would like to retain and take advantage of as much of this useful feature of object-oriented databases as possible.

We now explain the process that converts queries with shortcuts to SQL queries.

Given a path expression a.p, if a neither has an attribute called p, nor has a function called p whose input is of the type a, then there are two choices.[11]

- The 'a' in a.p has an attribute called 'Core' on which p is defined. In that case we replace a.p by a.Core.p in the whole query.

   It is easy to see that we use this step in Example 1 and 3.

- We have the clauses a is a subtable of a_1, a_1 is a subtable of a_2, ..., a_{n-1} is a sub-table of a_n in our schema such that p is either an attribute of a_n or is defined on a_n, and p is neither an attribute and nor it is defined on $a_1, \ldots, a_{n-1}$. In that case we re-place $a.p$ by $a_n.p$ in the query, add $a.k = a_n.k$ (where, k is the key of the relations $a_1, \ldots, a_n$) to the WHERE clause of the query and add a_n to the FROM clause of the query.

   It is easy to see that we use this step (with slight generalization) in translating Q_A to Q_B and Q_C to Q_D.

In the above we assume that a table is not a subtable w.r.t. two different tables.

2.3. Semantics issues: Can relations be object classes?

It has been pointed out, particularly by Date and Darwen [6] that semantical problems arise when relations are treated as object classes. For example, Consider a relation P with attributes W and V, and a relation Q with attribute X, Y and Z. Let us also assume that the type of W is integer and the type of V is the class corresponding to relation Q. Now suppose the tuples of relation Q are $\{(a, b, c), (d, e, f)\}$. The question is what does a tuple of the relation P look like. Is $(1, a, b, c)$ a possible tuple of P? The answer is no, since P only has two attributes.

We can avoid the above problem by associating with each relation R, a class C_R, and a constructor f_R. We say $(a_1, \ldots, a_n)$ is a tuple of R iff $f_R(a_1, \ldots, a_n)$ is a member of the class C_R.

With respect to relations P and Q, $(1, a, b, c)$ is not a possible tuple of P, while $(1, f_Q(a, b, c))$ is. When we just say that relations can be thought of as classes we are taking liberty with the syntax. This is fine as long as the semantics is made clear. That is what we have tried to do here. We would like to point out that similar concerns have been expressed during the discussion [1, 22] regarding merging of OQL and SQL3.

3.   A design methodology for MMDB

In this section, we describe a methodology for designing multimedia and semistructured databases, based on the approach of using ER diagrams as a first step in designing relational databases.

First, we will introduce an extension of the ER diagram, called *Core-ER diagram*, for the conceptual design of multimedia and semistructured databases. Then we describe how to to obtain a Core-ORDB schema from the Core-ER (CER) diagram.

3.1.   Core-ER diagram for multimedia and semistructured databases

We extend the ER diagram to account for multimedia and semistructured databases. We call it a CER diagram. The CER diagram is an extension of ER diagrams, and hence has all the features[12] of ER diagrams. The main addition is to the notion of entities. For example, an entity **Movie** has attributes such as title, producer, director, etc., that correspond to the abstract concept of a movie. But at the same time it also has a blob which is the movie itself. In our extension entities may have an *abstract* part and a *real* part. We are now ready to describe a CER diagram.

1. *Entities:*   Entities are represented by either a rectangle or by a rectangle containing an oval. We call the first "abstract entities", and correspond to entities in traditional ER diagrams, and the second "core entities". In this case, the outer enclosure (rectangle) corresponds to the original meaning of an entity in an ER diagram, while the inner enclosure (oval) represents the *real or the core entity*. In figure 1, **Movie** is a **core entity**. The entity **Employee** in figure 2 is an **abstract entity**. We would say simply "entity" or "entities" when something applies to either a "core entity" or an "abstract entity", or when the actual nature of the entity is clear by its context.

   The intuition behind this distinction is simple: for abstract entities, such as **Employee** in figure 2, we are not storing the real employee in our database, while for core entities (which might also be called "real entities"), we do store the actual (digitized) entity.

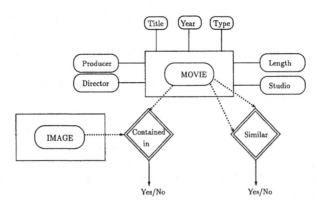

Figure 1.   The **Movie** core entity.

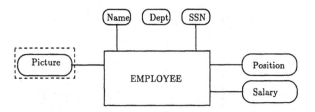

Figure 2.   The **Employee** abstract entity.

Intuitively, any object (entity) that is in digital format may be represented as a core entity.

2. *Attributes*

- *Conventional attributes* are represented as in ER diagrams. In other words, they are represented by an oval associated to the outer closure of an entity. All attributes of the entity **Movie** in figure 1 are of this type.
- *Unconventional attributes* of an entity are represented by an oval inside a dotted rectangle. The attribute **Picture** of the entity **Employee** in figure 2 is of this type. The dotted rectangle suggest that the picture has no abstractions. In presence of abstractions it is like another entity.

3. *Methods* (also referred to as functions or operators) are represented by diamonds (with a double enclosure, as opposed to diamonds with single enclosure for relationships) which have dotted arrows coming in and one solid arrow going out from it. The arrows represent the inputs and output of a method, respectively. The incoming arrows may either come from the inner enclosure (oval) of an entity or may come from the outer enclosure (rectangle) of an entity. When they come from the inner enclosure, it means that method uses the real entity as an input. For example, in case of figure 1, the method Contained_in uses the movie itself as one of the inputs. On the other hand, we may have a method *similar_credential* (not shown in figure 1) that takes input as the abstract attributes of two members of the entity movie and outputs a boolean value. A definition of this method could be: "Two movies have *similar credentials* if they have the same director, they were made in the same decade, either their producer or their studio is the same, and they are of the same Type." For this method the input arrows will come from the outer enclosure of the entity **Movie**.

4. *Keys and Relationships:* Keys and relationships are represented exactly as in ER diagrams. (Note that to easily distinguish between relationships and methods, we use diamonds with one enclosure for relationships, and two enclosures for methods. Also, incoming arrows to methods are dotted while all connections to relations are solid.)

Notice the basic difference between methods and attributes: values of attributes are stored and the values returned by methods are not stored; rather they are evaluated at runtime.

Example 5.   The CER diagram consisting of the **Employee** and **Email** tables and a 1-to-*n* relationship between Employee and Email is given in figure 3.

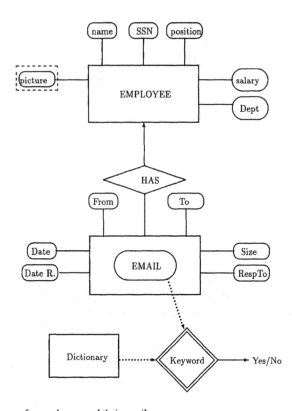

Figure 3.   CER diagram for employees and their emails.

3.2.   *From a CER diagram to a Core-ORDB schema*

It is obvious that if we remove the additional features (w.r.t. an ER diagram) from a
CER diagram we obtain an ER diagram. We refer to it as the *embedded ER diagram* of
a CER diagram. We now present an algorithm to construct a Core-ORDB schema from a
CER diagram.

1. For each abstract entity create a relation with its associated attributes as is done when
   translating an ER diagram. Unconventional attributes are treated the same way as conventional ones. For example, from figure 3 we create the relation *EMPLOYEE(Name,
   Dept, SSN, Position, Salary, Picture)* corresponding to the entity EMPLOYEE.
2. For each entity represented as a rectangle containing an oval create a relation with its
   associated attributes together with one additional attribute named *Core.* For example,
   the relation *EMAIL(emailID, from, to, size, date, resp_to, date_resp, Core)* is created
   corresponding to the entity EMAIL.
3. For each double diamond create a method definition[13] using as input the starting point of
   the incoming dotted lines, be it a core entity or one or more attributes of the abstraction

44

of a core or abstract entity.[14] For example, the following method definition is created for the entity EMAIL.

> FUNCTION Keyword(email,charstring)
> > RETURNS boolean
>
> <function definition>;

4. Obtain the embedded ER diagram from the given CER diagram and create tables corresponding to the non-ISA relations in the standard way. For the CER diagram in figure 3, there is only one relationship: HAS(SSN, emailID) where emailID is the key of the relation EMAIL.
5. For each IS_A relationship from an entity E_1 to an entity E_2, E_1 is a subtable of E_2.
6. Keys are defined as in the embedded ER diagram, except that for entities with two enclosures the attribute 'Core' (normally containing a pointer to the real entity) can be a key.

So, the complete Core-ORDB schema for the CER diagram in figure 3 is as follows.

> EMPLOYEE(Name, Dept, SSN, Position, Salary, Picture)
> EMAIL(emailID, From, To, Date, Size, Resp_To, Date_Resp, Core)
> HAS(SSN, emailID)
> FUNCTION Keyword(email,charstring)
> > RETURNS boolean
>
> <function definition>;

Similarly, the CER diagram in figure 1 can be translated into the following Core-ORDB schema:

> MOVIE(Title, Year, Type, Producer, Director, Studio, Length, Core)
> IMAGE(Core)
> FUNCTION similar(movie1:movieblob, movie2:movieblob)[15]
> > RETURNS boolean
>
> <function definition>;
> FUNCTION contained_in(picture:gifblob, movie:movieblob)
> > RETURNS boolean
>
> <function definition>;

4. Modeling the WWW as a multimedia database

In this section, we show how our conceptual modeling methodology can be used to model the WWW as a multimedia database. We start with a CER diagram that is very close to the model used in [15].

The CER diagram in figure 4 has two entities, one of which is a core-entity. There is one relation and four methods. Note the distinction between the methods *contains* and

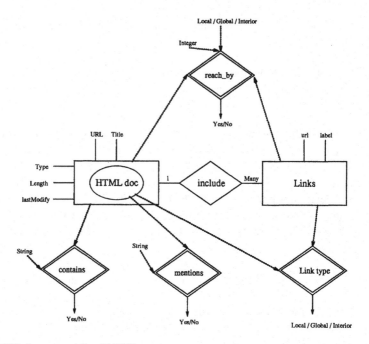

Figure 4.   CER diagram modeling WebSQL.

mentions. The input arrows of the method *contains* comes from the outer enclosure of the entity HTMLdoc and from 'String', while the input arrows of the method mentions comes from the inner enclosure (the core) of the entity HTMLdoc and from 'String'. The difference is that the method 'mentions' uses the 'core' while the method 'contains' uses one of the attributes of the abstraction: the title.

The Core-ORDB schema corresponding to the CER diagram in figure 4 has the following relations:

HTMLdoc(h_url,title,type,length,lastModify,core)[16]
Links(l_url,label)
Include(h_url,l_url)

and the following methods:

- **contains(HTMLDoc.Title, string):**   This method takes a string and the title of an HTMLdoc and finds out if the title contains the given string.
- **reach_by(HTMLDoc.url, url_to, by_n, l_type):**   Here, 'HTMLDoc.url' is the url corresponding to the HTML document and 'url_to' is a url; 'by_n' is an integer and 'l_type' can have the value, local, global or interior. This methods finds out if the url given by *url_to* can be reached from HTMLDoc.url given by after traversing at most *by_n* links of the type given by *l_type*.

- **mentions(HTMLdoc, string):** This method takes a string and an HTMLdoc and finds out if the HTMLdoc (its core) contains the given string.
- **linktype(HTMLdoc, url):** This method returns which type of link is the link specified by *url* w.r.t *HTMLdoc* (if any).

We now show how some of the queries from [15] can be expressed in an object-relational query language with respect to the above schema. We first give the query in English and then its representation in an object-relational query language.[17]

1. Find all HTML documents about "hypertext"

```
SELECT  HTMLdoc.h_url
FROM    HTMLdoc
WHERE   contains(HTMLdoc.title, "hypertext")
```

2. Find all links to applet from documents about "java"

```
SELECT  Links.l_url
FROM    HTMLdoc, Links, Include
WHERE   mentions(HTMLdoc, "java")
AND     HTMLdoc.h_url = Include.h_url
AND     Links.l_url = Include.l_url
AND     substring("applet", Links.label)
```

Note that *substring(instring, string)* is a standard method that searches for the occurrence of *instring* in *string*.

3. Starting from the Computer Science home page, find all documents that are linked through paths of lengths two or less containing only local links. Keep only the documents containing the string "database" in their title.

```
SELECT  Links.l_url
FROM    HTMLdoc, Links, Include
WHERE   substring("database", HTMLdoc.title)
AND     HTMLdoc.h_url = Include.h_url
AND     Links.l_url = Include.l_url
AND     reach_by("http://cs.utep.edu",Links.l_url,2,local)
```

4. Find all documents mentioning "Computer Science" and all documents that are linked to them through paths of lengths two or less containing only local links.

```
SELECT  HTMLdoc.h_url, Links.l_url
FROM    HTMLdoc, Links
WHERE   mentions(HTMLdoc, "Computer Science")
AND     reach_by(HTMLdoc.h_url, Links.l_url, 2, local)
AND     linktype(HTMLdoc.h_url, Links.l_url) = local
```

Note that we can use the 'recursion' feature of SQL3 to express queries that require the transitive closure of 'reach_by'.

In [15], the authors describe the query language WebSQL to express the above queries. The difference between our approach and the approach in [15] is that we use a general data model and a general query language. We must note that the WebSQL described in [15] is very useful and is implemented and we are not immediately planning to implement an alternative querying mechanism. We are only showing how the conceptual modeling methodology of this paper can be used to model the WWW as a database.

As in [15] the relations in our schema corresponding to figure 4 are virtual. The methods are supposed to be defined in the client site from where the query is submitted. However, in the future we can envision a combination of virtual and real schema, where some real data about the web pages may be specified as meta-information by the web masters of each site (and perhaps collected by some index servers), being used by a standard database query language (some extension of SQL). This is what we are advocating.

To give a flavor of our approach, we now extend the CER diagram in figure 4 to model additional features that will allow us to specify more sophisticated queries. The first extension is the CER diagram in figure 5.

The relations in the schema corresponding to the CER in figure 5 are:

HTMLdoc(*h_url*,title,type,length,lastModify,core)
WebObject(*w_url*,label,objectType,interactive,core)
Properties(*position,size,props*)

The properties relation is used to store the properties of a WebObject in an HTML document such as if it is an icon, a picture, a video or audio clip, a picture with a link etc.; and the size

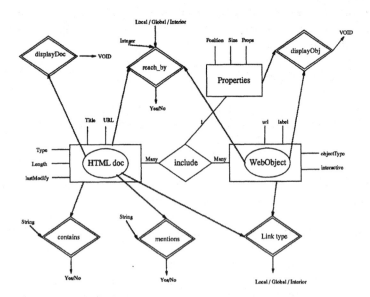

Figure 5.   CER diagram with 'uniform' WebObjects.

and position of the WebObject w.r.t. the document. The relation *include* now has additional attributes—the properties of an object in an HTML document, and it is now a many-many-1 relation.

include($h\_url, w\_url, position, size, props$)

We now have two additional methods:

- **displayDoc(HTMLdoc):** This methods displays an HTMLdoc.
- **displayObj(WebObject, Properties.position, Properties.size, Properties.props):** This method displays an web object in the position given by *position*, with size given by *size* and with properties given by *props*.

Using the above schema (corresponding to the CER diagram in figure 5) we can specify many additional queries such as:

- List all documents that have interactive web objects in them.
- List all documents that use the web object in *url* as an icon and also as a hot link.
- List all documents that have audio and video clips.
- List all documents that have a video clip or a picture labeled 'Clinton'.

The last query can be expressed as follow:

```
SELECT  HTMLdoc.h_url
FROM    HTMLdoc, WebObject, Include
WHERE   HTMLdoc.h_url = Include.h_url
AND     WebObject.w_url = Include.w_url
AND     (WebObject.objectType = "IMAGE"
   OR      WebObject.objectType = "VIDEO")
AND     WebObject.label = "Clinton"
```

The CER diagram in figure 5 does not completely distinguish between the different kinds of web objects. It uniformly[18] abstracts all the different type of web objects. This is similar to the approach in [13] and the detailed abstraction in it [13] can be easily added to figure 5.

To distinguish between different kinds of web objects we can introduce various subclasses to the class of web-objects. This is modeled as a CER diagram in figure 6. These subclasses may have abstractions and methods specifically applicable to them. In figure 6, we have shown some of the attributes of the entity IMAGE (a subclass of WebObject).

We could have methods such as the method 'Contained in' in figure 1 with inputs from IMAGE and VIDEO. We could further introduce classes such as 'aeroplane_image' as a subclass of 'IMAGE' and so on. The possibilities of enhancing the CER diagram in figure 6 is endless and our approach provides a conceptual tool to do that.

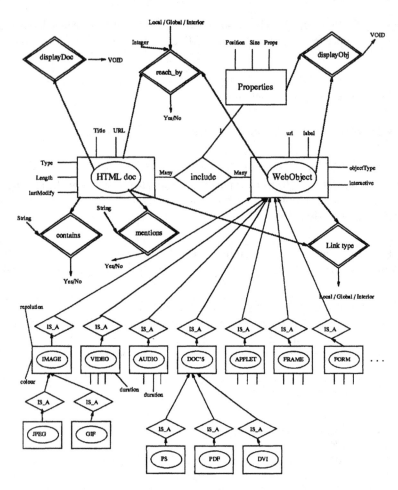

Figure 6. CER diagram with subclasses of WebObjects.

5. Displaying answers

One question that we have not addressed so far is how the answer to a query submitted to a multimedia database is presented to the user. In conventional databases, either the answer is presented as a table or the user writes display specifications in the embedding language (Visual Basic, C++, etc.) or in a report writing language. We believe that since multimedia databases may have web like front ends we should provide a simpler way for the user to specify display specifications.

We consider two different approaches: (i) Objects in general and multimedia objects in particular have a 'display' specification as part of the data definition. (ii) The display specification of the answer to a query is included with the query. The two approaches can work together if we assume that, if a display specification is given in the query, then it is followed, and if no display specification is given in the query, then the 'display' specification in the type definition of the object is used by default.

5.1. Display specification as part of the data definition

We suggest that 'display' be a reserved word in the data definition language which will be used in type or table definitions as a method that displays the corresponding object (or row object). Like other methods a type may inherit 'display' from its super types. In response to a query, even if 'display' is not mentioned in the query (as described in the next subsection) the final answer is passed on to the appropriate 'display' method to be displayed properly. As to exactly how this is implemented, it depends on the actual DDL implementation, and our idea is that it will follow the standard method definition of the DDL in question.

5.2. Display specification bundled with the query

We have designed and implemented a display specification language extension to SQL (SQL+D) [2] that will allow us to specify how the answer of a query posed to a multimedia database should be displayed. The whole language specification and architecture, and a comparative view of it in light of other efforts is too large to be part of this paper. We present here a few examples of display specifications using SQL+D to give a flavor of our approach.

Example 6.   Consider a database for a video rental store containing movie titles and other general information of the movies, plus a movie clip and a picture of the promotional poster. Also available is a list of the actors in a movie, and other information about the actors, including their picture. The schema looks as follows:

MOVIE	(available, title, director, producer, date, classification, rating, Core, poster)
MOVIE_ACTORS	(title, name, role)
ACTORS	(name, dob, biography, picture)

where all the attributes of **MOVIE_ACTORS** and all the attributes of **MOVIE** are character strings, with the exception of *Core*, which is a video (mpeg or avi), and *poster*, which is an image (in tif, gif, jpeg or any other standard image format). The attributes *name*, *dob* and *biography* in **ACTORS** are also character strings, *biography* being a long (memo) field, and *picture* is an image.

We would like to pose the following queries:

1. List all actors in "Gone With the Wind" with their pictures and biographies.
2. Display all action movies and their posters, allowing to play the movie if desired.

The first query would look as follows after it is translated to **SQL+D**:

SELECT	MOVIE_ACTORS.name,
	ACTORS.biography,
	ACTORS.picture
FROM	MOVIE_ACTORS, ACTORS
WHERE	MOVIE_ACTORS.title = "Gone With the Wind" AND
	ACTORS.name = MOVIE_ACTORS.name
DISPLAY	PANEL main, PANEL info ON main(*east*)
WITH	MOVIE_ACTORS.name AS *list* ON main(*west*),
	ACTORS.picture AS *image* ON info(*north*),
	ACTORS.biography AS *text* ON info(*south*).

Query 1. Querying the actors in "Gone With the Wind".

This is a standard SQL query up to the **WHERE** clause, thereafter the **DISPLAY** clause is used to specify where data is to be placed on the screen. Since the DISPLAY clause operates on the **data extracted** from the query, only the attribute names included in the **SELECT** clause can be used inside the **DISPLAY** clause.

The list of **PANEL** declarations following the **DISPLAY** keyword constitute the layout statement, and determine the overall layout of the screen: PANEL main is always the first and represents the whole screen or window where the query answer is being displayed, and the panels that follow (like "info", in the above example) are positioned within "main" or within other panels as specified by the **ON** subclause (in the example, the panel "info" is positioned on the west side of "main"). The panels listed here will contain different data display elements, specified in the **WITH** statement that follows.

The **WITH** statement contains a list of display specifications, indicating the kind of display element (like image, text, button, and others) desired for each attribute in the SELECT clause and their relative location within the panels previously defined in the layout statement. By default, if the user does not specify how to display all the attributes, the values of the attributes that have no display specification are grouped and displayed as a table in the south-most and east-most panel (lower right).

This query will display, as shown in figure 7, a scrollable list of the actors on the west half of the screen, and a panel on the east half containing a picture at the top and the actor's biography at the bottom. The picture and biography displayed correspond to the currently selected tuple from the answer set.

The "currently selected tuple", is in a sense a pointer, which at first points at the first tuple in the answer set. Thereafter, the user can move through the answer set by using one of the four master control buttons displayed on the main panel: one each to move the pointer to the previous tuple and the next tuple, plus two that allow jumping to the first or last tuple in the answer set. The tuples are sorted by the attribute indicated by the user in the (regular) SQL "ORDER BY" and/or "GROUP BY" clauses, if any.

In addition, there are ways to control navigation via the displayed data directly, as is the case of a list or through the use of the keywords **ALL** or **ALL DISTINCT**, explained later. In a list, the value of all the tuples for a particular attribute are listed (the names of the actors, in the above example), and the user can select any tuple simply by clicking on a particular item on the list. If this is done, the pointer in the answer set is moved to the tuple that contains the selected attribute.

Figure 7. Display generated by Query 1.

The user has visual cues in all the displayed elements that indicate which is the selected tuple. For example, in a list, the current tuple is highlighted in reverse video.

It is a good practice to display the key attributes of the relation as a list, whenever possible, to make navigation easier. That way, the user can see some portion of the data in advance and go directly to the tuple of interest, instead of blindly going tuple by tuple until the correct one is found.

The second query, to display all action movies and their posters, allowing to play the movie **if desired**, will be written as follows in **SQL+D**:

```
SELECT    title, poster, core
FROM      MOVIE
WHERE     classification = "Action"
DISPLAY   PANEL main, PANEL b ON main(east)
WITH      poster AS image ON main(west),
          title AS list ON b(north),
          "Play" AS button ON b(south)
              TRIGGER 'mpegplay(' + core + ')'
```

Query 2. Query to see the poster of action movies and play a selected movie at will.

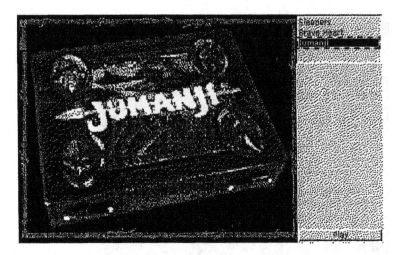

Figure 8. Display generated by Query 2.

The display corresponding to this query is shown in figure 8. The north, south, east, and west locations are sized automatically to fit the data displayed on them.

Since the button labeled "Play" has a **TRIGGER** associated to it, double clicking on the button causes an associated command to be executed. **SQL+D**, the associated command is indicated in the **TRIGGER** portion of the display specification.

A **TRIGGER** associates either a query or an executable program to a particular attribute or display element. The associated query or application is invoked when the element that contains the **TRIGGER** is double clicked. The **TRIGGER** keyword follows an attribute or fixed label specification and is followed by the name of a stored query or an executable ("mpegplay", in the above example) and a list of parameters to be passed to it (the value of the attribute video_clip, above).

For example, if the user were to double click on the "Play" button while "Jumanji" was highlighted on the list, the following command will be triggered:

mpegplay(jumanji.mpeg)

assuming the value of the video_clip attribute of the tuple that contains "Jumanji" is "jumanji.mpeg".

When database attributes are listed as parameters to queries or executables, the value of the attribute(s) when the TRIGGER is invoked is(are) passed to the associated query or executable. The value of the attribute is determined by the current tuple selected in the display.

The video clip could be played directly upon selection of the tuple, by substituting the last attribute specification in the **WITH** statement by the following: **video_clip AS video ON b(south)**

In this case, the user would be presented with a video display element in the bottom half of panel **b**, with the standard command buttons "Stop", "Play", "Pause", "FF", "RW" found in any video player.

However, since the query intended to let the user decide when to load the video rather than load it automatically for display, we must use the button as a display element and trigger the video player only when the user clicks on the button. This feature allows fast retrieval of tuples for navigation, loading "heavy"[19] attributes only when the user wants to see them. The same technique could be used for attributes that contain images, audio, postscript documents, or any other element which takes longer to load than text.

We will now introduce a more extended example application, which we have implemented.

Example 7. The database contains the campus map, plus maps of each floor in the different buildings on the UTEP campus. For each building, some pictures are available, together with a list of rooms, their descriptions, and their corresponding coordinates in the floor map. There is also some additional information and/or the http address of an associated home page (if available) for some of the data items in the database. This information is in free-text format, and includes historic highlights or detailed directions to reach the buildings, and the home pages correspond to the people, organizations, offices or departments that occupy the rooms listed.

The database schema is as follows:

CAMPUS	(campus_area, campus_area_map)
BUILDING	(building_name, building_picture, campus_area, coordinates)
FLOOR	(building_name, floor, floor_map)
ROOM	(building_name, floor, room_name, description, home_page, detail_info, coordinates)

To this schema, a user can pose queries that will let them find a particular place on campus, but also there are many (common) queries predefined and available.

For example, the following predefined query allows to view the main campus with a list of all of the buildings, as shown in figure 9:

SELECT	CAMPUS.campus_area_map,
	BUILDING.building_name
FROM	CAMPUS, BUILDING
WHERE	CAMPUS.campus_area = "Main Campus"
DISPLAY	PANEL main
WITH	BUILDING.building_name AS list ON main(east),
	CAMPUS.campus_area_map AS image ON main(west)

Query 3. Query to display area map and list of buildings in the Main Campus.

In addition, if we want the buildings to be outlined on the map (polygons drawn over the building in green), we can use the coordinates attribute (adding it to the **SELECT** clause). It contains a series of x, y coordinates for each vertex of the polygon that outlines the building (or room, in the ROOM relation), and substitute the **DISPLAY** clause in the previous query

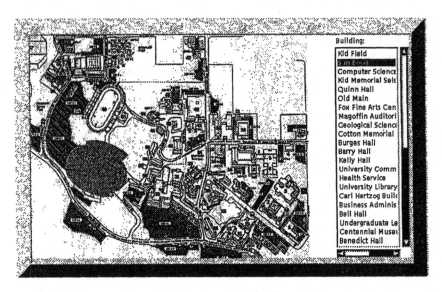

Figure 9.   Display generated by Query 3.

by the next clause:

    DISPLAY   PANEL main
    WITH   building_name AS list ON main(east),
              CAMPUS.campus_area_map AS image ON main(west)
              ALL BUILDING.coordinates AS polygon ON main(west)

The keyword **ALL** indicates that all the attribute values of "BUILDING.coordinates" in the answer set are to be shown at the same time.

As the user navigates through the answer set, the polygon corresponding to the selected tuple (building), will be filled in red (or reverse video). The rest of the polygons (non-selected) will remain unchanged, to give a visual cue as to which tuple (building) is currently selected. If the user clicks on one of the polygons, the corresponding building will be highlighted on the list. Thus, the **ALL** keyword turns any display element into a virtual "list" in the sense the user can navigate through the answer set via the displayed elements, just as if they were displayed in a list.

Specifying the same location for both the coordinates and the area_map indicates that the elements should be overlaid. Overlaying order follows the order in which the elements are specified in the **DISPLAY** clause.

The idea of overlaying can be extended and applied for such things as overlaying subtitles in English over a movie with audio in Spanish. This is more complex, however, as it would require matching subtitles to the corresponding frames in the movie. But it might be practical for short video clips in a language course, for example.

Now, if we want to trigger a separate query to explore a building, we change the display specification for building_name to the following:

building_name **AS** list **ON** main(east)
    TRIGGER 'building_maps(' + building_name +')'

where the symbol '+' indicates concatenation with the actual value of the attribute building_name at run time, when the user clicks on the corresponding element on the list.

The query to start exploration of a building is stored as *building_maps*, receives as input parameter the name of a building, and is written in **SQL+D** as follows:

```
SELECT    BUILDING.building_name,
          BUILDING.building_picture,
          FLOOR.floor
FROM      BUILDING, FLOOR
WHERE     BUILDING.building_name = + input + AND
          FLOOR.building_name = BUILDING.building_name
DISPLAY   PANEL main, PANEL b ON main(south),
WITH      building_picture AS image ON main(north),
          building_name AS title ON main(north),
          ALL floor AS button on b(east) TRIGGER
            'floor_buildings(' + building_name + ',' + floor + ')'
          "Select Floor to Visit" on b(west)
```

Query 4. Query to display the building picture and buttons to go to different floors.

Here, "input" is the name of an input variable that the query receives when it is executed, in this case, the building name. It results in the screen shown in figure 10.

The triggered query, **floor_buildings**, looks as follows:

```
SELECT    FLOOR.floor_map, ROOM.floor,
          ROOM.room_name, ROOM.detail_info,
          ROOM.home_page, ROOM.coordinates
FROM      FLOOR, ROOM
WHERE     FLOOR.building_name = + input_1 + AND
          FLOOR.floor = + input_2 + AND
          ROOM.floor = FLOOR.floor
DISPLAY   PANEL main,
          PANEL b on main(west),
          PANEL c on main(east),
          PANEL d on b(south)
WITH      floor_map AS image ON c(north),
          ALL coordinates AS poly ON c(north),
          room_name AS list ON b(north),
          detail_info AS text on b(center),
          ALL DISTINCT floor AS button on c(south)
            TRIGGER 'floor_buildings(' + building_name + ',' + floor + ')'
          home_page AS button on b(south)
```

Query 5. Query to display the floor map and a list of rooms, plus extra information.

Figure 10.   Display generated by Query 4.

It receives two input parameters: the building name and the floor. This is a more elaborated query, since now the trigger makes a recursive call. In **SQL+D**, recursively calling a query is possible since now the same query is invoked, but with new parameters, and the display changes to show the changing data. The generated display is shown in figure 11.

6.   Related work and future directions

Our work is a first step towards general and systematic design and modeling of multimedia and semistructured databases. In the past several specific designs have been suggested [8, 15, 16, 18]. For example, in [15] WebSQL a query language with respect to a virtual web database is presented. We believe it is important to focus on general approaches. In [13], a general approach to design multimedia databases is presented, but it proposes a completely new model. Our goal has been to stay close to standard models (ORDB, OODB), particularly to relational model.

Recently, there has been a trend towards object-relational databases. Very few papers have been published on this topic though. As evident from our approach we believe it (with

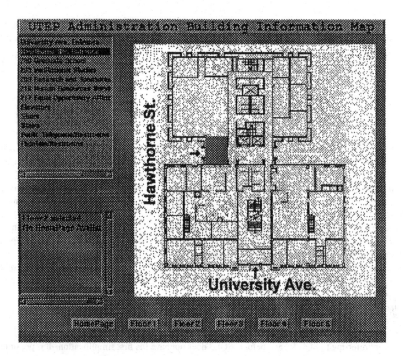

Figure 11.   Display generated by Query 5.

certain modifications) to be suitable for multimedia databases. In the text of this paper we have used features from SQL3 and the data model of Illustra. Most ORDB models focus more on complex types than on multimedia databases. For example, Stonebraker in his book [19] has significantly more examples dealing with non-multimedia complex data than on multimedia data. *In this paper our main concern is multimedia data and thus we have consciously overlooked non-multimedia complex data.*

In the future we would like to continue further on our proposed approach. In particular, we would like to immediately pursue, query optimization, combining relations, and making it easier for the user to ask a query. With respect to query optimization, we need to prioritize different selections. In general, less expensive selections should be done before more expensive selections. For example, equality and inequality based selections may need to be done before selections involving similarity between pictures.

In conventional database design, after ER diagrams are converted to relations, certain relations can be combined. We need to do the same with respect to the CER diagrams. But we need to be careful about the meta-data (particularly, the subclass informations). For example, when the ER diagram (in [20]) about Employees, departments, and managers is converted to relations we have the relations EMPS(ename, salary), MANAGER(ename), DEPTS(dname, d#), MANAGES(ename, dname). The last three are later merged to a single relation DEPTS(dname, d#, manager). If this was a CER diagram, we will also have *MANAGER* is a subtable of *EMPS*, which is affected by the merging and we need to change it to *DEPTS.manager* is a subtable of *EMPS*. This is used in Example 4.

One of our goals is to make it easier for a user to ask a query. Particularly, we would like the user to be able to ask a query even if he/she is not completely familiar with the schema. In this paper we have taken a few steps on this direction. We can further improve our approached by allowing incomplete path expressions [9, 10, 21].

Notes

1. We are also concerned about representing and querying semistructured and unstructured data. A list of such data includes: Emails, News postings (semistructured ascii); Programs in a computer language such as, C, C++, Java, etc. (semistructured ascii); Newspaper articles, and free text (almost unstructured).
2. A multimedia repository is basically a collection of multimedia artifacts, with very limited querying ability.
3. This can be generalized to any artifact, including multimedia artifact and artifacts abstracted in conventional databases.
4. This is also true for conventional databases. For example, when the IRS investigates a corporation, it looks beyond the database of the company (like at other computer files, invoices, account statements, reports, and other documents) to find information not in the database.
5. Most observations about SQL3 in this paper are based on articles about SQL3, i.e., based on secondary sources. We have been unable to obtain the authentic SQL3 document, although we did consult the SQL-92 book [14].
6. With merger of object-oriented and relational models [22] this may not remain a drawback.
7. Another possible name for this attribute could be 'self'.
8. Unless we are talking about science fiction.
9. Here we are referring to SQL-92 and before. SQL3 does not have the first simplification. It is possible that it has the second.
10. For example, Kifer et al. in [11] say the following to contrast relational databases with object-oriented database:
    "The central feature of the relational data model is that data is conceptually grouped by properties. For instance, information regarding a given person may be scattered among different relations, such as employee, manager, and project. In contrast, object-oriented representation seeks to group data around objects ... and the user can access, directly or by inheritance, all public information about any object once a 'handle' for the object is obtained."
11. We assume that our language is designed such that both choices are not applicable.
12. For brevity we do not discuss weak entities. We intend to treat them as done in ER diagrams with minor changes.
13. Note that by using CER diagram instead of ODL definitions, we not only make the schema visual but also we do not have to repeat methods with respect to each object type whose elements can be one of the inputs to the method.
14. Here, the abstraction that can be depicted reflects only the distinction between having as input the core entity or one or more of its attributes. For simplicity in the diagram, exactly which attributes from the abstraction are passed is not specified. This would need to be defined when the diagram is translated to actual functions.
15. We do not actually get the data types of movie1 and movie2 from the diagram, but from knowledge about the nature of the core entity *MOVIE* that the database designer has. We include the data types here for clarity.
16. We are using h_url and later l_url to distinguish the attributes HTMLdoc.url and Links.utl, respectively.
17. Here we are following the notation of Illustra.
18. V.S. Subrahmanian introduces the principles of autonomy, uniformity and hybrid organization for organizing multimedia data in his forthcoming book on multimedia databases. While the CER diagram in figure 5 corresponds to his principle of uniformity, the CER diagram in figure 6 corresponds to hybrid organization.
19. By "heavy" we mean attribute values that are of a significantly larger size than the rest of the attributes of the tuple.

References

1. F. Bancilhon and A. Carlson, "Providing rich query functionality—SQL3 discussion paper," ISO/IEC JTC1/SC 21/WG3 DBL LHR, ASC X3H2-95-462, Dec. 95.
2. C. Baral, G. Gonzalez, and T. Son, "A multimedia extension to SQL," Technical Report, Dept. of Computer Sc., University of Texas at El Paso, 1997.
3. C. Batini, S. Ceri, and S. Navathe, "Conceptual Database Design: An ER Approach," Benjamin/Cummings, 1992.
4. D. Beech, "Collections of objects in SQL3," in VLDB 93, 1993, pp. 244–255.
5. R. Cattel (Ed.), The Object Database Standard: ODMG—93, Release 1.2, Morgan Kaufman, 1996.
6. C.J. Date and H. Darwen, "The third manifesto," ACM SIGMOD Record, Vol. 24, No. 1, 1995.
7. C. Faloutsos, Searching Multimedia Databases by Content, Kluwer Academic Publishers, 1996.
8. M. Flickner et al., "Query by image and video content: The QBIC system," IEEE Computer, Vol. 28, No. 9, pp. 23–32, 1995.
9. G. Gonzalez, "Intuitive querying in object oriented databases," M.S Thesis, Department of Computer Science, University of Texas at El Paso, 1994.
10. Y. Ioannidis and Y. Lashkari, "Incomplete path expressions and their disambiguation," in SIGMOD, 1994, pp. 138–149.
11. M. Kifer, G. Lausen, and J. Wu, "Logical foundations of object-oriented and frame-based languages," Journal of ACM, 1993, to appear.
12. F. Manola and J. Sutherland, SQL3, in ANSI X3H7 Object Model Features Matrix, http://info.gte.com/ftp/doc/activities/x3h7/by_model/SQL3.html
13. S. Marcus and V.S. Subrahmanian, "Foundations of multimedia information systems," JACM, May 1996.
14. J. Melton and A. Simon, Understanding the New SQL: A Complete Guide, Morgan Kaufman, 1992.
15. A. Mendelzon, G. Mihaila, and T. Milo, "Querying the world wide web," Technical Report. Univ. of Toronto, 1996.
16. V. Ogle and M. Stonebraker, "Chabot: Retrieval from a relational database of images," IEEE Computer, Vol. 28, No. 9, pp. 40–48, 1995.
17. P. Sistla, C. Yu, and R. Haddad, "Reasoning about spatial relationship in picture retrieval systems," in VLDB 94, Santiago, Chile, 1994.
18. R. Srihari, "Automatic indexing and content-based retrieval of captioned images," IEEE Computer, Vol. 28, No. 9, pp. 49–56, 1995.
19. M. Stonebraker, Object Relational DBMSs, Morgan Kaufmann, 1996.
20. J. Ullman, Principles of Database and Knowledge-Base Systems, Computer Science Press, Vol. 1, 1988.
21. J. Van den Bussche and G. Vossen, "An extension of path expressions to simplify navigation in object-oriented queries," in Proc. Deductive and Object Oriented Databases, 1993, pp. 267–283.
22. Drew Wade, SQL3/OQL Merger, May 1996. http://www.jcc.com/sql_odmg_convergence.html

Chitta Baral is an Associate Professor of Computer Science at the University of Texas at El Paso. He did his undergraduate degree ('87) in Computer Science and Engg. from IIT, Kharagpur and his M.S. ('90) and Ph.D. ('91) from the University of Maryland, College Park. His interests are in the areas of multimedia databases, deductive and active databases, knowledge representation, logic programming, nonmonotonic reasoning, reasoning about actions and updates, and cognitive robotics. He received the NSF research initiation and CAREER awards in 1992 and 1995, respectively, and has published 50 conference and journal articles.

Graciela Gonzalez is currently a Ph.D. candidate at the University of Texas at El Paso, and is developing computer-related educational television programs, incorporating WebTV content. Her primary research areas include Multimedia Databases, Database Theory, and Workflow. From 1992 to 1997 she worked for EDM International as a Software Engineer, leading development in Imaging and Workflow Systems. She received a Masters Degree in Computer Science in 1994, and has taught classes in Data Structure and Database Theory at UTEP.

Tran Cao Son is a Ph.D. student in Computer Science at the University of Texas at El Paso. Prior to the Ph.D. program, he has worked as System Analyst and Programmer for six years. During this time he has helped developing a number of database systems. His current research interests include agent theories, nonmonotonic reasoning formalism, multimedia databases, knowledge representation, and action theories.

Multimedia Tools and Applications 7, 67–82 (1998)

QOS-aware Middleware for Mobile Multimedia Communications

ANDREW T. CAMPBELL   campbell@ctr.columbia.edu
The COMET Group, Center for Telecommunications Research, Columbia University, Room 801 Schapiro Research Building, 530 W, 120th St., New York, NY 10027-6699
http://comet.columbia.edu/~campbell, http://comet.columbia.edu/wireless

Abstract. Next generation wireless communications system will be required to support the seamless delivery of voice, video and data with high quality. Delivering hard *Quality of Service (QOS)* assurances in the wireless domain is complex due to large-scale mobility requirements, limited radio resources and fluctuating network conditions. To address this challenge we are developing *mobiware*, a QOS-aware middleware platform that contains the complexity of supporting multimedia applications operating over wireless and mobile networks. Mobiware is a highly programmable software platform based on the latest distributed systems technology (viz. CORBA and Java). It is designed to operate between the application and radio-link layers of next generation wireless and mobile systems. Mobiware provides value-added QOS support by allowing mobile multimedia applications to operate transparently during handoff and periods of persistent QOS fluctuation.

Keywords: middleware, mobile communications, adaptive algorithms, active transport, QOS

1. Introduction

Recent years have witnessed a tremendous growth in the use of wireless communications in business, consumer and military applications. The number of wireless services and subscribers has expanded with systems for mobile analog and digital cellular telephony, radio paging, and cordless telephony becoming widespread. Next generation wireless networks such as *wireless ATM (WATM)* will provide enhanced communication services such as high resolution digital video and full multimedia communications.

The main challenge in a combined wireline/wireless ATM networks derives from *complexity*. Complexity is present in various forms in mobile multimedia communications. First, the combination of multi-rate multimedia connections with mobility proves difficult to achieve in practice. A connection with certain capacity reserved at a particular cell may have to be re-routed when the mobile device changes its location. The new path to the desired location may not have the original required capacity. Therefore, re-negotiation of resources allocated to the connection is needed. At the same time, the flow (e.g., audio or video) should be transported and presented 'seamlessly' to the destination device with a smooth change of perceptual quality. This motivates the need for QOS with mobility.

Next, audio and video flows are characterized by the production, transmission and consumption of single media streams (both unicast or multicast) with associated QOS. For multicast flows, individual receivers (both wired and wireless) may have differing capability to consume flows [20]. This could be due to either fluctuating network resources with mobility or imposed by individual applications. Bridging this heterogeneity gap [9] in mobile multicast environments [6] while simultaneously meeting the individual mobile devices' QOS requirements is an area of research that remains to be resolved.

Third, radio channel's varying QOS characteristics and device mobility, fundamentally impact our ability to deliver hard QOS guarantees in the WATM environment. QOS controlled mobility and a QOS adaptive transport system share a common link in that they must be able to respond or "adapt" to the changes in the delivered quality due to QOS-fluctuating wireless channel or application-level mobility, respectively.

In this paper, we propose a unique solution to the overall problem of complexity that is based on a methodology of networking programming based on a QOS-aware middleware platform called *mobiware*. We extend an open control methodology that has been previously developed at Columbia [14] to control ATM networks to the mobile ATM domain. The basic tenet of this methodology is to separate the network hardware from software.

The structure of this paper is as follows. Section 2 presents an overview of mobiware and its architecture which provides a framework for network programming and adaptation of flows. Following this we describe a set of adaptive and active algorithms which lay at the heart of mobiware's adaptation strategy. We describe a QOS controlled handoff algorithm in Section 3, an adaptive and active transport algorithm in Section 4 and an adaptive network service in Section 5. Finally, in Section 6 we provide some concluding remarks.

2. Mobiware: Programmable mobile networking

Mobiware is a software middleware platform that runs seamlessly on mobile devices, base stations and mobile-capable ATM switches. The platform is built on distributed system and Java technology and incorporates new architecture and novel adaptive algorithms to support QOS controlled mobility. The goal of the mobiware adaptive algorithms is to transport scalable flows, reduce handoff dropping and improve wireless resource utilization. We use the term "controlled QOS" in this paper to distinguish it from hard QOS guarantees offered by fixed ATM networks. Implicit in the term is the notion that flows can be represented and transported as multilayer scalable flows at mobile devices. Adaptive algorithms help scale flows during handoff based on the available bandwidth and an application-specific *flow adaptation policy* [7]. This policy characterizes each audio and video flow as having a minimum QOS layer and a number of enhancements.

Mobiware provides a highly programmable platform for ease in the service creation, monitoring and adaptation of multimedia flows. The concepts of programmability and adaptability are fundamental when addressing the complexity of supporting mobile multimedia applications over QOS-varying mobile networks. By adaptability we mean as mobiles roam mobiware's adaptive algorithms conspire to scale flows to match available bandwidth at the bottleneck node, e.g., the base station. By programmability, we mean that mobiware's APIs are 'high-level' enough to allow adaptive algorithms to be implemented using distributed systems technology.

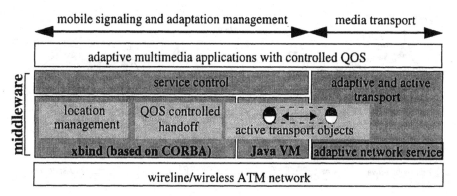

Figure 1. Mobiware architecture.

2.1. Architecture

Mobiware promotes the separation between mobile signaling and adaptation management on the one hand and media transport on the other. As illustrated in figure 1 mobiware utilizes xbind (based on CORBA) and Java for signaling and adaptation management during handoff or periods of persistent QOS fluctuation. The Java Virtual Machine executes on mobile devices, base stations and mobile-capable ATM switches and supports the dynamic execution of *active transport objects (ATOs)*. These transport objects constitute an 'active' component of the mobiware transport system which can dispatch ATOs to strategic points in the network or end-systems to provide value-added QOS support. The concept of ATOs is derived from work on protocol boosters [11].

The realization of end-to-end QOS control and the exploitation of scalable flows is achieved in mobiware through; (1) resource binding between mobile devices, base stations and ATM switches; and (2) provision of a set of QOS-aware adaptive algorithms. These algorithms operate in unison under the control of mobiware:

- *QOS controlled handoff*, provides signaling for handoff which exploits the use of: (1) soft-state and hard-state to represent flows; (2) aggregation of flows to/from mobile devices; and (3) routing and QOS renegotiation anchor points to limit the impact of small-scale mobility on the wider fixed network;
- *adaptive network service*, provides hard QOS guarantees to base layers (BL) and soft QOS guarantees to enhancement layers (viz. E1 and E2) of multimedia flows based on the availability of resources in the wireless environment; and
- *adaptive and active transport*, supports the transfer of multilayer flows through the provision of a QOS-based API and a set ATOs (e.g., media scaling [9]) and *static transport objects (STOs)*, e.g., playout control. STOs are statically configured and execute at mobile and fixed devices only. In contrast, ATOs are dynamically dispatched to the mobile devices, base stations or ATM switches to support valued-added QOS at strategic nodes.

Media scaling plays an important role in processing flows on-the-fly to match available resources at a bottleneck node, e.g., the air-interface. Media scaling exploits the

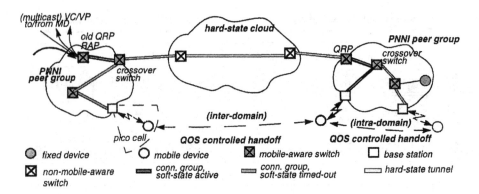

Figure 2.   QOS controlled handoff.

intrinsic scalable properties of multi-resolution audio and video flows. In addition, adaptive algorithms take into account the knowledge of the user's flow adaptation policy to actively *filter* flows at critical nodes. This is achieved using an adaptive and active transport system to dispatch media scaling agents called *mobile filters* at critical nodes in the network or end-systems. Mobile filters are one of a class of ATOs which best utilize the available bandwidth to seamlessly deliver media with smooth change in the perceptual quality during handoff. Mobiware updates a location management algorithm during handoff. The mobiware location management uses a logical-name-to-logical-name mapping to express the current position of each mobile device.

The mobiware platform models the wireless portion of the ATM network as being divided into pico-cells each served by a base station connected to a wired ATM network as illustrated in figure 2. Base stations are cell relays which translate the ATM cell headers from radio ATM format to that used by standard ATM. Each base station supports signaling, QOS control and adaptation of flows based on semantics of an adaptive network service. The existing wired ATM network provides connectivity between base stations. We organize the wireless network into domains. A domain consists of a set of base stations which are under the management of mobile-aware ATM switches. A domain corresponds to a logical partition of the wireline network and the physical location of the base stations in hierarchies for scalable routing (in ATM Forum PNNI routing, these domains are peer groups).

3.   QOS controlled handoff

The goal of the QOS controlled handoff algorithm is to dynamically re-route a set of connections associated with a mobile device from one base station to another without significantly interrupting flows in progress. The design of QOS controlled handoff is driven by two conflicting design goals: (1) support mobility; and (2) minimize the impact that small scale mobility has on the wireline portion of the network during handoff. To achieve these two design goals we introduce:

- *mobile soft-state*, models the dynamics of mobility through the continuous re-routing and QOS re-negotiation of flows as a mobile device roams. Soft-state is established between a per mobile *QOS re-negotiation anchor point* (*QRP*) and the mobile device. Hard-state is used between the QRP and the fixed network portion of the network;

• *connection group* (*CG*), provides a common routing representation for all virtual paths and virtual circuits destined to/from the same mobile. Connection groups decouple handoff re-routing from resource allocation at a per mobile *routing anchor point* (*RAP*). The RAP allows collective control and mobility management of all flows associated with a mobile device during handoff. Having a single reference point to manage all connections greatly simplifies handoff; and

• *logical anchor points*, provide an interface between the hard-state and soft-state portions of flows. The RAP and QRP are logical anchor points which localize the periodic re-routing and re-negotiation and during handoff processing, respectively.

Mobiware allows collective control and management of all connections associated with a mobile device using a single connection group identifier (CGI), which uniquely represents a single reference point to manage all connections. Connection groups are setup using multicast connection management operations, e.g., *addBranch* to a connection group tree. Removing a branch of a connection group tree after handoff is managed automatically through the semantics of the soft-state operations used in the mobile environment.

Mobiware handoff achieve this through the interaction of distributed QOS handoff algorithms with a set of mobiware *virtual resource objects* which model physical hardware devices and QOS as CORBA objects [19]. Mobiware models base stations [6] as a set of virtual resource objects: *virtualBasestation*, which is used to represent and manipulate the GCI/VP/VC routing table; *virtualWirelessLink*, which is used to represent and allocate QOS to a flow based on the concept of a *scheduler region* [14, 16]; and *virtualQOSFilter*, which is used to scale media at the base-to-mobile link.

In the following sections we will step through the QOS controlled handoff. See figure 3 for illustration of the handoff phases.

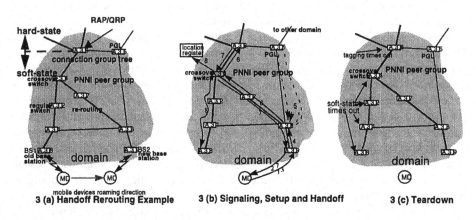

Figure 3. QOS controlled handoff walk-through.

3.1. Signaling phase

The first phase of QOS controlled handoff (see figure 3(b)) determines whether a new base station can provide a stronger signal at the desired level of QOS. A QOS monitoring algorithm resident at mobile devices monitors beacon messages which are periodically broadcast by all neighboring base station. In addition to indicating the strength of neighboring base station signals beacon messages indicate the residual capacity currently available at base stations. By periodically monitoring beacons from all neighboring base stations the mobile device is able to determine link qualities and occupancy of adjacent base stations and use this QOS state information as a basis to initiate handoff after a suitable dwell time.

The next phase of handoff is the establishment of a new signaling channel between the mobile device and the new base station. A mobile device issues a (1) signalRequest to the new base station over a dedicated meta signaling channel using the base station address found in the beacon message. This results in the creation of the signaling channel when the base station responds with a (2) signalResponse. The signaling channel carries all signaling and QOS management messages between the mobile and wireline network.

3.2. Setup phase

Once the signaling channel has been successfully created the mobile device initiates a forward handoff to the new base station. It does so by issuing a (3) *reservation message* (for details on the *res* message see Section 5) which includes connection group route state information and desired QOS required. The handoff management algorithm located at the new base station uses this state information to establish a new branch (between the crossover switch and new base station) to the existing connection group tree with the desired QOS. Mobile devices express desired QOS in terms of the semantics of the adaptive service and connection groups. Connection group QOS requirements are specified in terms of connection group base layer requirements and enhancement layer requirements, respectively. Admission control located at the new base station first determines whether sufficient resources are available to support the requested handoff.

Reservation messages can be updated by the distributed handoff algorithm as they are forwarded from the new base stations toward the rendezvous switch based on the availability of resources at the traversed nodes. The semantics of the adaptive service provide hard guarantees to the base layers and admit enhancements layers based on the availability of residual resources; that is, the resources remaining once all base layers have been guaranteed. The new base station only drops the handoff (*handoffDrop*) if insufficient residual capacity is available to meet the group connection base layer resource requirements. Assuming that sufficient resources are available to meet the minimum QOS requirements, the *res* message is routed toward the crossover and rendezvous switch reserving resources on route. Connection group routing information is used in combination with PNNI routing to determine (5) the shortest path between the new base station and the existing connection group tree which meets the desired QOS reflected in the *res* message. The PNNI peer group leader is interrogated (5) should the mobile device roam outside the current peer group domain of the old base station. This may suggest that the existing RAP would provide a sub-optimal routing point and a new RAP along with a new QRP is required. Generally, the new QRP is located close to the mobile device, and over a longer timescale a RAP re-routing algorithm determines when and where to move the RAP.

In the case where roaming is within the current peer group domain, the new base station issues a (6) *res* message to the crossover point. Each intermediate switch on route between the base station, crossover point and QRP provides admission testing and resource reservation. The QRP terminates QOS re-negotiation. The existing connection group traverses the crossover switch. Generally, the crossover switch processes the *res* message and forwards it to the rendezvous switch which also processes it and then responds by sending an (7) *adaptation message* (for details on the *adapt* message see Section 5) to the mobile via crossover and the new base station. The adapt message is used to commit switch and base station resources at the downstream nodes for the new connection group branch. Once the base station receives the adapt message it commits resources and broadcasts the adapt message to all mobile devices in the cell.

3.3. Handoff control

The adapt message serves two purposes. First, it confirms the level of QOS provided by the new base station and wireline portion of the network to the new mobile device as it enters a new cell. Second, it informs existing mobile devices of any resource changes which may have occurred during handoff to accommodate the new mobile device. The semantics of the adaptive service state that base layer resource reservation requests receive precedence over requests for any higher layer qualities. To this extent the quality delivered above the base layer to existing mobiles may be altered to allow a new mobile device to enter a new cell.

The handoff algorithm interacts with the media scaling agents (which interact with mobile filters—see Section 4.2) at the base station and QRP during connection group setup. The level of media scaling is dependent on the current utilization of the wireless link, application specific desired QOS and the semantics of the adaptive service. Media scaling may result in the "scaling-down" of mobile delivered quality when a mobile device enters a pico-cell and "scaling-up" when they leave. Mobile devices upload Java-based mobile filters (see Section 4.2 on active transport objects) to the base station or rendezvous switches in the case where the requested QOS could not be supported. This results in enhancement layers being dropped or filtered at specific points on a connection group tree (e.g., at the new base station or QRP). QOS filters support the delivery of different combinations of layers to particular mobile devices based on the available resources. Network-based mobile filters are essential to support multicast QOS to heterogeneous receivers.

Handoff registers new mobile devices with the domain location management which in turn allocates a new proxy ATM address as mobile devices roam into cells within a new peer group domain. A (8) *locationUpdate* message is used to register the mobile devices at the home location in this case and update the cache register at the old base station (8). QOS controlled handoff is based the notion of soft-handoff for roaming mobile receivers and hard-handoff for roaming mobile senders. In the case of soft-handoff, the mobile device simultaneously interacts with the old and new base stations. Once the QRP responds with an adapt message to the mobile device it begins to forward the new flow to the mobile. This results in duplicate cells (for old and new flow) arriving at the mobile device via the old and new base stations. The rendezvous switch uses cell tagging to preserve ATM cell level sequence integrity at the mobile device during handoff.

After tagging has commenced, mobile devices determine suitable synchronization points between old and new flows and initiate flow switching from the old to the new flow. After flow switching the old flow is rendered redundant. Old flows continue to arrive at the mobile devices as long as the route between the old base station and QRP is active; that is, old flows are switched through to the mobile while the mobile soft-state is still installed and has not timed-out. Mobile devices do not, however, have to process old flows.

3.4. Teardown

After flow switching the new base station refrains from sending any further periodic *res* messages to the old base station and closes the signaling channel to the old base station. Once the mobile soft-state timer expires the old branch of the connection group tree between the QRP to the old base station is timed out and removed; i.e., after the mobile soft-state timer expires resources are deallocated and switching tables flushed accordingly. This is defined as teardown.

Media scaling is once again invoked at the old base station to determine if deallocated resources can be utilized by any existing mobile devices at the old base station. Mobile devices located at the old and new base station periodically probe the base station and network for more resources using the *res* and *adapt* message pairs. During handoff, mobile devices resident at the old base station issue reservation messages toward the QRP and receive an adapt message which indicates any extra resources made available after a mobile has left the current cell. The new adapt message reflects any new resource availability and adjusts any QOS filters via interaction with media scaling agents at the old base/rendezvous switch. We describe the condition whereby resources freed up during handoff are distributed to remaining mobile devices at the old base station as scaling-up.

4. Adaptive and active transport system

A fundamental aspect of our work is the development of an adaptive and active transport that incorporates a QOS-based API and a full range of transport algorithms to support the delivery of continuous media over mobile networks. The mobiware transport operates in two modes:

- *adaptive mode*, which provides a set of STOs (viz. playout control, flow control, flow scheduling and shaping, flow monitor and adaptation manager) that best assists multi-media applications when adapting to minor QOS fluctuations as a consequence of cell/packet loss and delay variation; and
- *active mode*, which provides a set of ATOs (viz. mobile filters [2], mobile error control [12] modules and mobile snoop [3] modules) that can be dynamically dispatched to mobile devices, base stations or mobile-capable ATM switches to provide value-added QOS during conditions of persistent QOS fluctuation that may emerge during handoff.

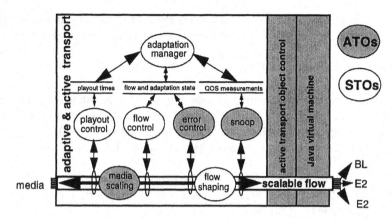

Figure 4.   Adaptive and active transport system.

In the active mode, a local adaptation manager monitor the loss available bandwidth characteristics of flows and interact with ATO control to select, dispatch, bootstrap, configure and tune the appropriate ATO to the requesting target node.

4.1.   Transport API

The transport API formalizes the end-to-end QOS requirements of the adaptive multimedia application (client or server) and the potential degree of media scaling acceptable to the application [7] (based on flow adaptation policy) which bounds its perceptual range. As illustrated in figures 1 and 4, applications interact directly with the service control API to establish, control and maintain the requested service. The service control algorithm governs the point at which a QOS controlled handoff is initiated.

The adaptive transport API assumes a client-server model where servers interact with service control to create *QOS groups* specifying their *QOS profile* (i.e., QOS requirements: traffic class, delay and bandwidth) for each multi-resolution of the flow and *flow adaptation policy* (i.e., the type of coding and prioritizing of the various resolutions used, and flow-spec for each flow) of the source media. The traffic class and delay bounds are common for each resolution of the scalable flow. The user can prioritize connections so that during handoff certain connections receive preferential treatment over others in light of reduced bandwidth (e.g., drop the video connection before the audio). The bandwidth for each resolution is specified in a flow-spec [7] by the clients and servers. Clients join QOS groups, inspect the QOS profile of the source and then select the appropriate resolutions by matching their capability to consume source media. For full details on the adaptive algorithms and API see [7].

4.2.   Active transport objects

Adaptation managers operate on all mobile devices, base stations and mobile-capable ATM switches and continuously monitor the performance of the channel and each flow.

Adaptation managers and QOS controlled handoff algorithms interact with local ATO control to request the remote loading of ATOs to support QOS during periods of service degradation.

Currently mobiware supports three types of ATOs:

- *mobile filters*, which are used during periods of limited bandwidth to either drop layers of a flow (we call these types of mobile filters media selectors) or process audio and video in the compressed domain to meet an available bandwidth [2, 10, 20]. In general, mobile filters are dispatched once during handoff and are tuned based on the available bandwidth;
- *mobile error control modules*, which provide hybrid ARQ and FEC mechanisms for improved reliability of audio, video and data over the air-interface during periods of excessive cell/frame loss [12]; and
- *mobile snooping modules*, which help increase the performance of flows (e.g., TCP data flows) by snooping [3, 12] end-to-end protocol messages as a means to trigger the local value-added error control mechanism over the air-interface.

ATO are application specific and interact with differing algorithms to provide value-added support. For example, mobile filters are driven by an available bandwidth indication and interact explicitly with the adaptive network service algorithm. In addition, "*ATO state*" can be transparently moved during handoff. For example, a mobile filter executing on a base station can be automatically moved and reconfigured at the new base station. Movement of ATO state like this is dependent of the specific ATO and the operating conditions existing in the new cell. ATO state can propagate along with the connection state from the old to the new node over the wireline portion of the network. In this case the ATO state can take advantage of the wireline ATM interconnect to achieve a fast handoff. ATOs are capable of flexible autonomous actions in QOS fluctuating environments. Operationally, ATOs can be dispatched, configured and executed at any ATO-capable networked node.

4.3. Active transport object management

ATO management consists of a distributed algorithm which manages the installation of new ATOs anywhere in the network. ATO management uses a client-server approach to select, dispatch, bootstrap, configure and tune new ATOs between an ATO server and the target node.

As illustrated in figure 5 ATO management is divided into three operational modes:

- *ATO control* is a distributed signaling algorithm which comprises mobiware ATO control objects. These objects are permanently resident at the base stations, mobile capable ATM switches and mobile devices. ATO control objects support a set of methods to *select* (1), *dispatch* (2) and *configure* (4) mobile filters;
- *ATO instantiation* fetches remote Java bytecode classes (which are representations of ATOs) and *bootstraps* (3) them into Java VM environment based at base stations or mobile capable ATM switches. Once an ATO has been loaded and booted into a switch

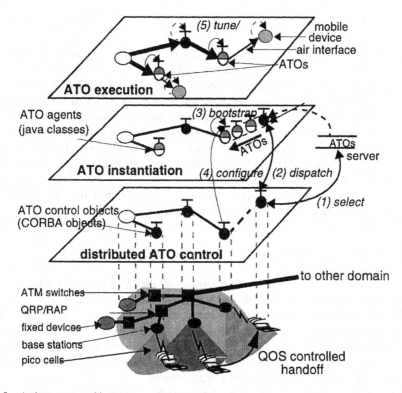

Figure 5. Active transport object management.

or base station the local ATO control object initiates a configure (4) operation to complete the instantiation phase; and

- *ATO execution and tuning*, at this point ATO can act autonomously to provide value-added QOS support to the transport of continuous media or data. Some ATOs interact with existing algorithms during the execution phase and can be periodically tuned (5).

As illustrated in figure 4, the adaptation manager periodically monitors the QOS delivered at the channel. In the case where the platform needs value-added software. Mobile filters are capable of flexible autonomous actions in QOS fluctuating environments. Operationally, mobile filters can be dispatched, configured and executed at the base stations or ATM switches. Mobile filters can be periodically tuned via a filter interface to match the available resources at a particular bottleneck node (e.g., base station or mobile capable ATM switches). In addition to being QOS adaptive, mobile filters automatically propagate during handoff. For example, in the case of a handoff between two WATM radio ports existing mobile filters (called *mobile filter state* in mobiware) propagate along with the connection state from the old to the new base station over the wireline portion of the network. In this case, the mobile filter state can take advantage of the wireline ATM interconnect to achieve a fast handoff.

4.4. *Mobile filter ATOs*

Currently we have implemented a media selector ATO in Java that drops either E1 (i.e., P pictures) and E2 (i.e., B pictures) frames of an MPEG-1 stream based on the available resources. Media selectors ATOs do not process the media unlike other computationally intensive mobile filters e.g., dynamic rate shaping mobile filters [10]. One of the key performance issues related to mobile filter technology is the time taken to dispatch, bootstrap and configure new agent over wireless and wireline interfaces. Another important performance concern relates to the performance penalty paid by flows as they are processed at ATM switches and base stations. The amount of delay introduced by such operations as flows traverse ATO is dependent on the computational complexity of the ATO, the additional overhead of the Java VM and the cost of derailing ATM cells for filtering. For some initial performance results relating mobile filter ATO see [2, 12].

5. Adaptive network service

The adaptive service is based on previous work on adaptive service for wireline ATM networks first proposed in [7]. This service model provided "hard" guarantees to the base layer (BL) of a multilayer flow and "fair share" guarantees to each of the enhancement layers (e.g., E1 and E2) supported by the service. To achieve this, the BL undergoes a full end-to-end admission control test [7]. In contrast, enhancement layers were admitted without any such test but competed for residual bandwidth with all other adaptive flows which traversed a particular switch along a specific route.

Similar schemes have subsequently been adopted by a number of practitioners in the wireless communications field [4, 5]. However, one drawback of these adaptive service schemes is that a QOS fluctuation at a particular switch (e.g., due to a new call being admitted) in a wireline/wireless environment can potentially impact other flows traversing the link/port. This results in a chain-reaction as distributed adaptive resource management algorithms resolve the new change in state. Unbounded adaptive service will typically occur in highly QOS fluctuating environments such as in mobile wireless systems. Therefore, there is a need to bound this chain-reaction while at the same time offering an adaptive service to mobile terminals to reduce the probability of handoffs being dropped as new mobiles roam into a bottleneck pico-cell.

This is the motivation behind our adaptive service. The adaptive service primarily operates over the wireless segments of end-to-end flows; that is, between the QRP, base station and the mobile devices as illustrated in figure 2. Therefore, QOS adaptation is limited to the pico-cellular area and does not directly impact the wired portion of the network. Mobile devices compete for wireless resources by interacting with an adaptive service algorithm at the base station. This limits adaptation to where it is more likely to occur: at the wireless link between the base station and QRP. Enhancement layers are rate controlled based on explicit feedback mechanisms about the current state of the ongoing flow and the availability of residual bandwidth at a base station.

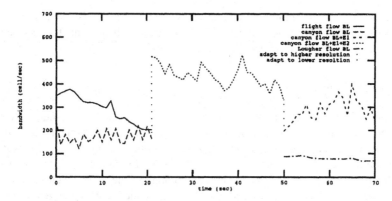

Figure 6.   Scalable video flows.

A number of objectives motivate the design of a new wireless adaptive service for mobile QOS fluctuating networks. The first objective is to admit as many base-layers as possible across the wireless link. As more base-layers are admitted the guaranteed capacity region grows to meet the hard guarantees for all base signals. In contrast, the residual capacity region shrinks as enhancement layers compete for diminishing residual bandwidth resources. Our second objective is to fairly share this wireless residual capacity among competing enhancement layers based on an algorithm called *weighted fairshare* [7]. In addition, another associated objective is to limit the impact of the wireless adaptive service on the wired network. Our fourth objective is to adapt flows both discretely and continuously based on an adaptation mode supplied in the user-supplied adaptation policy. In the discrete mode, no residual bandwidth is allocated by the wireless adaptive service algorithm unless a complete enhancement can be accommodated. In contrast, in continuous mode any portion of the residual capacity can be made available and be utilized by the adaptive flow [6].

Figure 6 illustrates the operation of the adaptive service over a wireline ATM link. The bandwidth of the link which the adaptive algorithm shares between three different video flows (akin to mobile devices) was setup to be similar in bandwidth capability to a low bandwidth wireless ATM link (e.g., admission control is preset to 600 ATM cells/s to be shared by all competing flows). The scenario shows the consumption of three video clips beginning at time zero. The *canyon* and *flights* video flows start at time zero and only have their BL supported; i.e., the minimum quality is provided. No residual capacity is available to support higher qualities because of the limitation of the available resource (i.e., 600 cells/s). At 20 s into the trace, the *flights* video flow terminates freeing up resources for remaining flows (i.e., remaining mobile devices). This is akin to a mobile device roaming out of a pico-cell. At this point the adaptive service attempts to switch into the higher resolutions for remaining flows. The trace shows that the *canyon* video flow receives the best quality (i.e., BL + E1 + E2) after the *flights* video terminates. This situation remains stable until another video flow starts up at 50 s into the trace which is akin to a mobile device roaming into the cell and competing for wireless link resources. Resources are thus allocated to meet the BL QOS requirements of the new mobile device. The *canyon* video flow is adapted down to the BL + E1 quality at 50 s into the scenario as a result of admitting the new flow (akin to a new mobile). While the scenario is taken from wireline ATM experimentation into adaptive services [7] the results indicate what the service would look like to mobile devices as they roamed between cells.

5.1. Mobile soft-state

Rendezvous switches serve as points above which re-routing and QOS re-negotiation only occur when a mobile device roams between two adjacent routing domains. Inter-domain roaming operates at a much lower frequency than intra-domain roaming. Occasional inter-domain roaming requires re-routing and QOS re-negotiation in the wireline network. We contain the frequency of re-routing and QOS re-negotiation caused by small-scale mobility from impacting the wider wireline network. This is contained at the QRP. Above the QRP only infrequent re-routing and QOS re-negotiation occur. Below the QRP (between the mobile devices and QRPs) frequent re-routing and QOS may be observed.

Based on our understanding of the dynamics of small-scale (intra-domain roaming) and large-scale (inter-domain roaming) mobility we model end-to-end flow through a combination of "hard-state" (above the QRP in the wireline network) and "soft-state" (below the QRP in the wireless network). We argue that soft-state is suited to support the dynamics of mobility and QOS adaptation found in wireless and mobile networking.

A significant contribution to our approach to handoff is the use of soft-state [21] to support the dynamics of mobility in the wireless and wireline network. Soft-state is used between the mobile devices and QRP because it best suits the dynamic nature of QOS adaptation and device mobility. Mobile devices periodically send reservation messages (res) toward the QRP in the wireline network. These reservation messages carry the mobile devices desired QOS requirement and are interpreted by the base station and fixed network infrastructure. Resources are allocated to the mobile device over a particular wireless/wireline route for the duration of the mobile soft-state timeout. If during that time the infrastructure receives another res message it refreshes the state held in the base station and switches between the mobile device and the QRP. As mobile devices roam between adjacent cells the periodic res messages are used by the mobile devices to establish a new state (i.e., a route with QOS attached) at the new base station and intermediate switches. In addition, as the mobile device roams into a new cell the old connection group soft-state times out and is deallocated automatically. The periodic res message is used in combination with an adapt message to continually probe the base station and network for better QOS.

6. Conclusion

This paper has introduced a QOS-aware middleware platform for mobile multimedia communications. Mobiware has been specifically designed to address the complexity of proving QOS support for adaptive multimedia applications over wireless and mobile networks. Mobiware includes two key attributes which contains complexity. These are programmability and adaptability. In this paper, we presented the key adaptive algorithms that govern the available strategies for adaptability in mobiware. These include a QOS controlled handoff scheme which promotes the use of soft-state, connection groups and logical anchor points for fast and seamless handoff. We have also described a new transport systems which utilizes adaptive and active transport objects to provide value-added QOS support in the end-systems and network. The final mobiware adaptive strategy is based of a novel adaptive network service which has been designed to provide hard QOS guarantees for minimum flow quality and best effort delivery for higher quality.

The mobiware testbed consists of 4 ATM switches (viz. ATML Virata, Fore ASX100/ASX200s, NEC Model 5, Scorpio Stinger) and 4 base stations. The base stations are multihomed 200 MHz Pentium with 25 Mbps wireline access to the wireline ATM network and 2 Mbps WaveLan air-interfaces to a number of mobile devices based on Pentium PCs and notebooks. The PCs run Linux, Windows/NT and xbind (based on CORBA). An early version of mobiware runs on PCs, base stations and the ASX100 ATM switch.

Finally, we have implemented a beta version of the handoff protocol which support soft-state, connection groups and logical anchor points [12]. In addition, we have completed the implementation of active transport object management and support mobile filters for media selection during handoff [8]. Currently we are implementing other adaptive and active transport objects and plan to investigate the integration of mobiware with wireless ATM radios. The results from this stage of our research will be submitted as contributions to the new IEEE standardization initiative on "Programmable Network Interfaces" [13].

Performance results of our experimental testbed can be found in [22].

References

1. C. Aurrecoechea, A.T. Campbell, and L. Hauw, "A survey of QOS architectures," Multimedia Systems Journal, Special Issue on QOS Architecture, 1996 (to appear).
2. A. Balachandran and A.T. Campbell, "Mobile filters: Delivering scaled media to mobile devices," Technical Report, Center for Telecommunications Research, Columbia University, Oct. 1996.
3. S. Balakrishnan, E. Amir Seshan, and R.H. Katz, "Improving TCP/IP performance over wireless networks," 1st International Mobile Computing and Networking (MOBICOM'95), Berkeley, Nov. 1995.
4. V. Bharghavan, "Adaptive resource management algorithms for mobile computing environment," Proc. OPEN-SIG Workshop, New York, April 1996.
5. K. Brown and S. Singh, "A network architecture for mobile computing," INFOCOM'96, San Francisco, March 1996.
6. A.T. Campbell, "Towards end-to-end programmability for QOS controlled mobility in ATM networks and their wireless extensions," Proc. 3rd International Workshop on Mobile Multimedia Communications (MoMuC-3), Princeton, Sept. 1996, and Wireless ATM Workshop, Espoo, Finland, Sept. 1996 (invited presentation).
7. A.T. Campbell and G. Coulson, "Implementation and evaluation of the QOS-A transport system," 5th IFIP International Workshop on Protocols for High Speed Networks, Sophia Antipolis, France, Oct. 1996.
8. A. Campbell, R.-F. Liao, and Y. Shobatake, "Using soft-state for handoff in wireless ATM networks," The Sixth WINLAB Workshop on Third Generation Wireless Information Networks, March 1997.
9. Delgrossi et al., "Media scaling in a multimedia communications system," ACM Multimedia Systems Journal, Vol. 2, No. 4, 1994.
10. A. Eleftheriadis and D. Anastassiou, "Meeting arbitrary QOS constraints using dynamic rate shaping of coded digital video," in Proc. 5th International Workshop on Network and Operating System Support for Digital Audio and Video, Durham, New Hampshire, April 1995, pp. 95–106.
11. D. Feldmeier, "Protocol booster," COMET Group Seminar, Feb. 1996.
12. http://comet.columbia.edu/wireless
13. IEEE Standardization Initiative on "Programmable Network Interfaces."

14. A.A. Lazar, S. Bhonsle, and K.S. Lim, "A binding architecture for multimedia networks," Journal of Parallel and Distributed Computing, Vol. 30, No. 2, pp. 204–216, 1995.
15. D.G. Messerschmitt, J.M. Reason, and A.Y. Lao, "Asynchronous video coding wireless transport," Workshop on Mobile Computing Systems and Applications, Santa Cruz, Dec. 1994.
16. M. Nagshineh and A. Acampora, "QOS provisioning in micro-cellular networks supporting multimedia traffic," INFOCOM'95, Boston, April 1995.
17. J. Porter, A. Hopper, D. Gilmurray, O. Mason, J. Naylon, and A. Jones, "The ORL radio ATM system, architecture and implementation," Technical Report, ORL Ltd., Cambridge, UK, Jan. 1996.
18. D. Raychaudhuri (NEC USA), L. Dellaverson (Motorola), M. Umehira (NTT Wireless Systems), J. Mikkonen (Nokia Mobile Phones), T. Phipps (Symbionics), J. Porter (Olivetti Research), C. Lind (Telia Research) and H. Suzuki (NEC C&C Research), "Scope and work plan for proposed wireless ATM working group," ATM Forum Technical Committee, ATM Forum/96-0530/PLEN, April 1996.
19. The Common Object Request Broker: Architecture and Specification, Revision 1.2, published by the Object Management Group (OMG) and X/Open, Dec. 1993.
20. N. Yeadon, F. Garcia, A. Campbell, and D. Hutchison, "QOS adaptation and flow filtering in ATM networks," in Proc. 2nd International Workshop on Advanced Teleservices and High-Speed Communication Architectures, Heidelberg, Germany, Sept. 1994.
21. L. Zhang et al., "Resource reservation protocol (RSVP)—version I functional specification," Working Draft, draft-ietf-rsvp-spec-07.ps, 1995.
22. Angin et al., "A programmable mobile network: design, implementation and evaluation," IEEE Personal Communication, 1998.

Andrew T. Campbell is an assistant professor in the Department of Electrical Engineering and member of the COMET Group at the Center for Telecommunications Research, Columbia University, New York. He is currently leading a research effort in Wireless Media Systems focusing on the development of QOS programmable middleware for mobile multimedia networks that comprise ad-hoc, broadband and next generation Internet technologies. Before joining academy Dr. Campbell spent 10 years in the industry focusing on the design and implementation of network operating systems and communication protocols for packet-switched local area and tactical wireless networks.

Multimedia Tools and Applications 7, 83–101 (1998)

BRAHMA: Browsing and Retrieval Architecture for Hierarchical Multimedia Annotation

ASIT DAN   asit@watson.ibm.com
DINKAR SITARAM   sitaram@watson.ibm.com
IBM Research Division, T.J. Watson Research Center, Hawthorne, NY 10532

JUNEHWA SONG   junesong@cs.umd.edu
University of Maryland, College Park, MD 20742

Abstract. Traditional browsing of large multimedia documents (e.g., video, audio) is primarily sequential. In the absence of an index structure browsing and searching for relevant information in a long video, audio or other multimedia document becomes difficult. Manual annotation can be used to mark various segments of such documents. Different segments can be combined to create new annotated segments, thus creating hierarchical annotation structures. Given the lack of structure in media data, it is natural for different users to have different views on the same media data. Therefore, different users can create different annotation structures. Users may also share some or all of each other's annotation structures. The annotation structure can be browsed or used to playback as a composed video consisting of different segments. Finally, the annotation structures can be manipulated dynamically by different users to alter views on a document. *BRAHMA* is a multimedia environment for browsing and retrieval of multimedia documents based on such hierarchical annotation structures.

Keywords: media annotation, retrieval architecture, hierarchically annotated media, video browsing and viewgroup management

1. Introduction

A picture is worth a thousand words.

Recent advances in computer and communication technology have made it feasible to support complex multimedia applications on each desktop [7–9, 14–16]. Users can compose and share multimedia documents consisting of fragments of media data stored in a large multimedia database [7, 15, 16] (see figure 1). In traditional multimedia applications, large video or audio files are played back sequentially. However, newer applications may require searching and retrieval of relevant fragments from these files. Pure content based browsing which analyzes the files online is limited by the computational overhead of such tasks [5, 11, 13, 17, 18]. Most of the proposed techniques for automatic analysis of video content are based on exhaustive comparisons of several physical features such as color and texture from sequences of video frames, and currently provide a limited set of content information such as shot changes, key frames, similarity of frames, or the existence of certain shapes. These methods require processing of huge amounts of data (half an hour of video data is 45 Mb even in 1.5 Mb/s MPEG 1 compressed format). Extracting more general

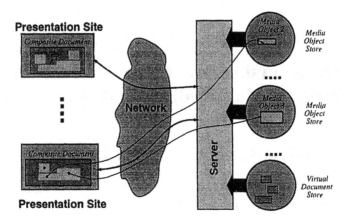

Figure 1.   Distributed multimedia environment.

content information that matches high level user perceptions (e.g., appearance or location of a specific person such as Clinton or Gore) is even more computationally intensive. Also, it is difficult to express complex abstractions or semantic information that may be present in a video segment (i.e., across multiple frames). Examples of such useful but complex abstractions are: training videos on a surgical operation or operation of a particular machine, audio signature of Vivaldi's *The Four Seasons*, etc.

Without structural information a large volume of data needs to be retrieved as well as searched based on the content. Manual annotation can be used to mark relevant segments for later retrieval [14, 16]. However, annotation can never capture all the details present in a media file. Therefore, different users may annotate the same or overlapping segments differently with what they see as important. Note that an important property of media data is *semantic continuity of data* which makes possible chunking of an arbitrary portion of a file in a meaningful way. This is unlike text based or other structured information (e.g., contrast a video segment to a set of records in a database).

Multiplicity of views.   As the previously mentioned proverb suggests, even a single picture carries a lot of information which cannot be expressed with a few words. Different users may be interested in different abstractions of the same picture frame. Even from an ordinary portrait of a person, one could see many different interpretations of his/her facial expression, physical attributes, fashion consciousness, and the surroundings in which the portrait was composed. The possible number of abstractions across multiple frames is theoretically unbounded. Therefore, it is natural to provide the means for diversity of expressions over the same media content.

Users may also share their views of relevant fragments with others. A user can further annotate existing segments, or create new virtual objects from many existing segments. Consider the following video conferencing example where people from various divisions of a corporation participated in a task-force to bring a new product to the market. Figure 2 shows a part of an example annotation hierarchy. The product to be marketed is composed of two components: Component A and Component B. Each component is again comprised of two

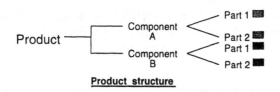

Product structure

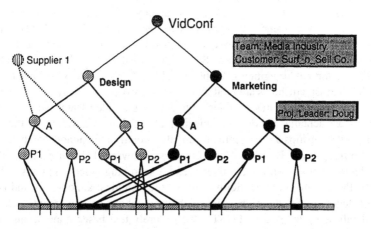

Figure 2.   Example annotation hierarchy: video conferencing.

parts, part 1 (P1) and part 2 (P2). The *design* team is more concerned with the schedules of various parts, while the *marketing* team participated in discussing the useful features. Each node in the hierarchy represents a view of a portion of the video stream. For later reviewing, the various teams annotated different segments of the unstructured conference, and created structured views. The view of the *marketing* team is represented by the portions with the thick lines in the graph. The product *design* team has annotated additional relevant segments discussing the schedules. Some of the product components have a dependency on *supplier* 1. Hence, a different view of the video conference is created for sharing with *supplier* 1.

In this paper, we propose the BRAHMA platform for supporting the applications of the type described above. The primary features supported in BRAHMA are dynamic creation, browsing, and sharing across multiple users of annotation hierarchies and playback of composed videos based on such hierarchies. Annotations in BRAHMA associated with a node consist of an *Attribute-Value* pair. Hence, the BRAHMA annotation structure is richer than a flat annotation structure as used in many current systems (e.g., digital library). Both the name of the attribute and the value are arbitrary strings. The hierarchical annotation structure facilitates sharing of views among multiple users and enriches the semantics of the video data. In the above example, *supplier* 1 and *design* teams share only a part of the annotation structure.

The rest of the paper is as follows. Section 2 describes the BRAHMA environment for creation and browsing of annotation structures and playback of composite media objects. Section 3 describes how BRAHMA facilitates sharing of multimedia information across users and maintains annotation structures internally. Section 4 discusses issues related to retrieval of composite media objects and delivery of such objects over the networks. Section 5 provides a summary and conclusions of this paper.

1.1. Contributions and relationship to other work

Video algebra for composition of videos using manually annotated segments is proposed in [16]. In BRAHMA, we extend this framework in several ways. First, BRAHMA accommodates sharing of views and different annotation structures for different users. The users can update these structures dynamically. Second, the attributes are dynamically chosen by users and hence, annotated segments can be identified by other users via *attribute synonym matching*. In contrast, attributes are predefined in currently proposed systems that maintain a database for storing attributes of video segments (e.g., Video Database Browser [14]). Once the database schemas are defined, it is difficult to add new attributes to the database. Additionally, relationships across segments are also stored in the annotation hierarchy. As mentioned above, the UC Berkeley Video Database Browser [14] is implemented using a meta-data database along with query interfaces for searching video segments. Therefore, unlike BRAHMA, it does not explicitly deal with hierarchical annotations and uses only predefined categories of annotations. Hence, their model can be implemented on standard relational database systems (e.g., POSTGRES). Purely text-based annotations that lacks *attribute-value pair* representation and hierarchical structure, limits the capability to query stored annotations. The contrast in the capabilities between the BRAHMA and the pure text based annotation systems is analogous to the contrast between the database systems and the file systems in terms of their query capabilities on stored textual data (e.g., *SQL* vs. *grep*).

A new data model for supporting video data types is proposed in [6]. The data model includes annotation for thematic indexing of video contents. However, the model accommodates annotations only for physical video segments (i.e., a set of frame sequences), but does not support hierarchical annotation structures. The annotation is also based on a predefined set of attributes that are specific to an application. Therefore, as in the case of video meta-data [14], it is hard to define attributes on the fly, and to accommodate the needs of diverse individual users. Using such a data modeling methodology (or the meta-data database) by creating different customized data models for different users will also result in replication of common information across users. More sophisticated schemes that factors out common information across a set of users (assuming such information can be identified a priori) will require (as in BRAHMA) an integrated access control mechanism.

A mathematical framework for multimedia database systems has been proposed in [10]. In their framework, the authors define a media-abstraction scheme on top of physical media representations (audio, video, etc.). The paper further defines a general purpose logical query language and indexing structure which is independent of the media instances. In this framework, a media presentation can be generated from a sequence of queries.

Finally, the nodes in BRAHMA are also different from structured objects with pre-defined attributes and classes, since the node attributes are defined dynamically by users to incorporate the diversity of possible semantics. Creation and maintenance of annotation structure in BRAHMA is similar in many ways to *schema evolution* in object-oriented databases. However, the annotation structure in BRAHMA is not predefined at any given time, whereas in OODB the focus is on adapting to the changing views via schema evolution of once defined object schemas. Other contrasting points are the usage of this structure (i.e., *attribute synonym matching*), frequent changes in annotation structures in BRAHMA and sharing of partial views.

2. BRAHMA user environments

As explained earlier, the applications being considered here will access a large volume of data. Automatic building of relationships across video segments is not suitable due to the high overhead and computational complexity in automatic extraction of features. Therefore, manual annotation of video segments is necessary. Additionally, different viewers may have different perspectives on the same video, and may want to create different manual annotations of the same video. Tools are needed for providing flexibility in creating such annotation structures. Note that manual annotation can be integrated with feature extraction as the lowest level of the structure built on a video.

BRAHMA provides various user interfaces (UI) to annotate a physical segment, to browse and/or update hierarchical annotation structure, to playback composite media objects and to build queries for composition and/or playback of new composite media object views. Multiple windows can be created to access different UIs simultaneously. Each UI window can also toggle between various UI modes.

2.1. Segment browser

The *Segment Browser* can be used to create or playback a physical segment node (figure 3). It also supports creation, modifications or browsing of the associated annotations. The Segment Browser is composed of a *frame viewer*, a *video scroll bar*, a *Segment property* pane and an *Annotation for segment* pane. The video scroll bar provides direct access to any video frame. A user browses a video sequence frame-by-frame using the scroll bar. A new segment is defined by clicking the NEW button and then by marking the starting and ending frames. The various properties (ID, VIEWGROUP, etc.) of this segment are then set on the "Segment property" pane. The annotations associated with this segment are defined in the "Annotation for segment" pane as ⟨attribute, value⟩ pairs. When a user selects an existing segment, it shows the currently defined ⟨attribute, value⟩ pairs. The properties of the segment as well as its associated annotations can be modified at this time. To aid users in this annotation process, a list of (possibly meaningful) suggested attributes can be loaded into the segment browser environment. Finally, by clicking one of the mode buttons (HIERARCHY BROWSER, COMPOSITE MEDIA BROWSER, QUERY BUILDER) the corresponding windows can be instantiated.

Random access to a MPEG compressed video frame.   One of the problems with MPEG compressed video sequences is the difficulty of direct access to a frame in the sequence. This is due to the inter-dependence of frames and predictive coding provided in MPEG. To

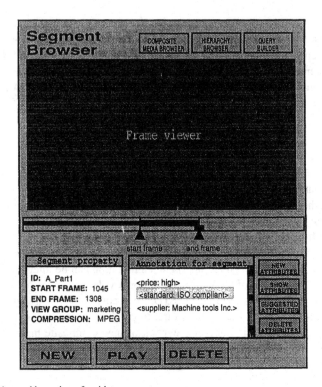

Figure 3. Creation and browsing of a video segment.

alleviate this problem, we use an associated non-MPEG auxiliary file that can be efficiently browsed frame-by-frame. The auxiliary file contains a reduced image sequence generated from the original MPEG compressed video sequence [17]. The reduced image sequence typically is 1/8 or 1/4 of the original size in both horizontal and vertical dimensions and hence, incurs a low storage overhead. Although it does not generate full resolution video frames, the reduced image sequence provides sufficient resolution to browse and annotate video segments. The generation of a reduced image sequence is very efficient as it is done entirely in the compressed domain.

2.2. *Hierarchy browser*

The hierarchical annotation structure in BRAHMA can be used to display the annotation hierarchy structure and to select a node (i.e., composite media object) for browsing its annotations. Users can also select a node for playback that results in playback of all associated segments in a pre-defined manner (i.e., according to pre-defined temporal and spatial relationships). A user may also browse the annotations associated with a selected node or navigate the hierarchy structure. Finally, a user can display/update the relationships across the component media objects of the current node.

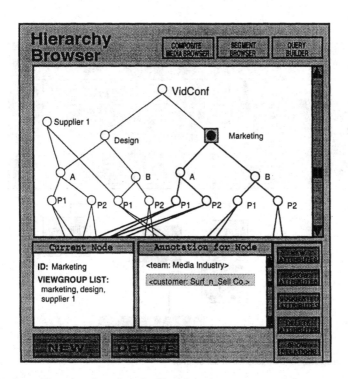

Figure 4.   Creation and browsing of an annotation hierarchy.

The creation and browsing of a composite object and its annotations are done using the *Hierarchy Browser* (figure 4). It is composed of panes for a *Hierarchy Navigator*, properties of the selected node (*Current Node*) and its associated annotations (*Annotation for Node*). The scroll bar as well as mouse clicks can be used to navigate the annotation hierarchy. A new node or composite media object is created by clicking the NEW button, and results in the creation of a new node in the "Hierarchy Navigator" pane. Various existing nodes can be linked (via the mouse) and made components of this new node. The properties of this new node are set in the "Current Node" pane. Similarly, properties of a selected existing node are displayed (and can be updated) in the "Current Node" pane. Annotations of the new node are created in the pane named "Annotation for Node". As before, annotations of a selected existing node can be updated in this pane. The "Annotation for Node" pane also allows creation of relationships across component nodes (see below). The various other buttons associated with this pane are self-explanatory.

2.3.   Structural relationships

Consider an example of three subsequent video segments which are annotated as ⟨*location* : *Bosnia*⟩ and ⟨*speaker* : *Clinton*⟩ as shown below. Using structural analysis of the video and using simple reasoning (that can be expressed via video algebra), it can be inferred that Clinton is speaking about Bosnia in the broader video segment.

Node Table

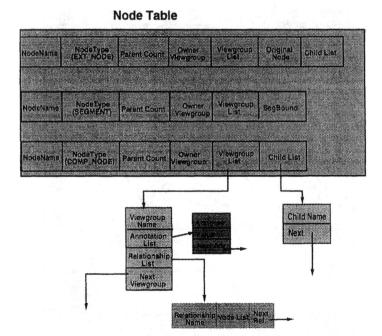

Figure 5. Data structures for maintenance of annotations.

```
          <location:    <speaker:     <location:
           Bosnia>       Clinton>      Bosnia>
    -----|----------|----------|-----------
```

From the above example, it is clear that the relationships across various segments or even sub-nodes contain important information. If such relationships are not explicitly stored, they have to be inferred. To avoid high computational overhead, such relationships need to be maintained explicitly. Some relationships may also be impossible to infer (as reasoned earlier for storing explicit attribute annotation). Consider another example of a medical instructional video, where various segments may refer to various phases of an operation. Here, the phases may be semantically related (e.g., opening or closing of a wound). The relationships across sub-nodes are stored as ⟨*RelationshipName, nodelist*⟩ (see figure 5).

2.4. Composite media browser

Playback of a composite media object and creation of display relationships amongst its components are described below. In a more elaborated case, a user can also create or display media objects by using a query. For example, a user may wish to retrieve all video segments containing songs by a specific singer, and create a new album with a particular theme and/or order. Video algebra can be used for this purpose [16].

Structural composition. Associated with a node in the annotation hierarchy are display relationships among its component nodes (which themselves may be atomic or composite media objects). When a media object is selected for playback its components are displayed according to these stored relationships. The structural composition includes both temporal and spatial relationships. For temporal relationships, we use Allen's interval algebra [1] which is summarized below.

- *before*(X,Y): Media object X is played before Y.
- *equal*(X,Y): Media objects X and Y are played in parallel.
- *meets*(X,Y): Media object Y starts when object X finishes.
- *overlaps*(X,Y): Media object Y starts while X is being played.
- *during*(X,Y): Media object Y starts after X starts and ends before X ends.
- *starts*(X,Y): Media object X and Y starts at the same time and X ends before Y ends.
- *finishes*(X,Y): Media object Y starts before X starts; X and Y end at the same time.

The spatial relationships can also be represented among media objects as following:

- rightOf (X, Y, *d*): Media object X is right of Y by distance *d*.
- below (X, Y, *d*): Media object X is below Y by distance *d*.
- topAlign (X, Y), bottomAlign (X, Y), leftAlign (X, Y), rightAlign (X, Y): Media object X and Y are aligned by the top, bottom, left, and right, respectively.

The sizes of individual display windows for component objects can also be specified explicitly.

Interactive browsing. As multimedia data involves visual or audio information, an efficient browsing capability is essential in effective management of multimedia data. This browsing capability needs to provide sufficient interactive capability such as fast forward, fast backward, pause, direct access to a specific frame, etc. The volume of multimedia data, however, makes it difficult to provide all such capabilities with full resolution.

3. Information sharing across users

The hierarchical annotation structure supported by BRAHMA can facilitate sharing of multimedia data as well as collaborative management of multimedia data. It provides a shared view of annotation and composite media objects by defining *viewgroups* for the hierarchy structure.

Viewgroup definition. A user can create a new viewgroup by claiming himself/herself as the owner of the viewgroup. He/she can also include other users and other viewgroups as members of the newly created viewgroup. Each member is granted selective permissions, i.e., browse privilege or browse/modify privilege of the structure and annotations. As a special viewgroup, the owner can include *public* as a member, which gives the access privilege to all users in the system. Each group member has the specified privilege to the annotation hierarchy of BRAHMA. Members with a browse privilege in a viewgroup can query and browse annotations or video segments which belong to the viewgroup whereas members with browse/modify privilege can also create/modify annotations or nodes for the viewgroup. However, maintenance of the membership of a viewgroup, for example, inserting a new group member, is performed by the owner of the viewgroup.

Media object sharing. The owner of an media object can grant permissions to any set of viewgroups during or after the creation of this new node or structure. There are four levels of access permissions granted to viewgroups:

View: The lowest level of access permission. The members of the viewgroup with *View* permission can browse and query over the current node and its subtree. However, no modifications of the annotation or the structure are allowed.

Append/Update: The members are allowed to append annotations to the current node and its subtree or delete appended annotations. However, no structural changes are allowed.

Extend: The members are allowed to append annotations and delete appended annotations to the current node and its subtree. The members are also allowed to Extend a node in the subtree by defining new nodes as children (see figure 7).

Copy: In addition to *Extend* permission, the members are allowed to copy a node and thereby define a new node. The member's viewgroup becomes the owner of the new node.

Note that a created node can only be deleted by its owner viewgroup. The access permissions of a specific member are determined by the combination of the access permissions to the viewgroup and the pre-defined role of the member within the viewgroup. For example, even if a viewgroup is granted an *Extend* permission to a particular node, all the members of the viewgroup with lesser privileges cannot exercise this permission. The owner or the members of the viewgroup with Extend privileges can add children to the specified node. However, the members of the viewgroup with only *Browse* permission can not extend the specified node, but can browse the extended nodes by other members of the same viewgroup.

A single user may belong to multiple viewgroups with different permissions allowed to the user within each viewgroup. During a user session, the user can select a list of viewgroups (out of the viewgroups associated with the user) as the currently selected viewgroup list (referred to as the *Current Viewgroup List*). Hence, this *current viewgroup list* defines the scope of the access and the user's current view of the annotation hierarchy. The access permissions available to a user is the union of the access permissions granted to this user based on its memberships to the viewgroups in the *current viewgroup list*.

During navigation of a structure, only the nodes visible to a user (based on his/her viewgroup memberships) are displayed. Similarly, the query operations are performed only on the structures accessible to a user. With an addition or deletion of a viewgroup to/from the *current viewgroup list*, the permissions and the visibility of the annotation hierarchy change. The system first resolves access permissions granted to an user based on the *current viewgroup list*. It marks the nodes of which the structural views have changed (due to the change in the *current viewgroup list*). The changed views of the nodes in the hierarchy can be instantiated (reflected to the browser and reflected to the query) by clicking the nodes or by a query.

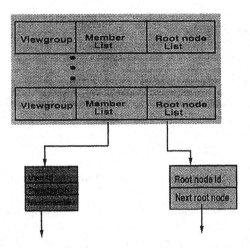

Figure 6.   Viewgroup table.

3.1.   Maintenance of annotation structure

The structures need to be manipulated dynamically: new nodes may be created, each segment or composed objects may be further annotated by new users, etc. Hence, the internal representation should provide support for efficient dynamic updates, look ups and video compositions. Below we describe the data structures used for maintenence of annotation structures and how these structures are used when creating a new node or modifying other aspects of the annotation structures. The system maintains two tables: the *Node Table* and the *Viewgroup Table* (see figure 6).

Figure 5 shows the Node Table, used to store the annotation structure. The Node Table contains an entry for each defined segment or composite object. There are three different types of nodes maintained in the Node Table:

Segment: The entry for a segment of a video consists of the Node Name, the Node Type (in this case, SEGMENT), a Parent Count which keeps track of the number of parents of a node, the Segment Boundaries, a Owner Viewgroup, and a Viewgroup List. The Segment Boundaries field contains the start and end of the segment together with the identifier of the video to which the segment belongs. The Owner Viewgroup is the viewgroup which created the current node and defines the access permissions to the node. The Viewgroup List contains, by viewgroup, a list of annotations on this segment and a list of relationships between this segment and other segments. Each viewgroup is allowed access to only those annotations and relationships, which are maintained in its Annotation and Relationship Lists. As described earlier, each annotation consists of an Attribute-Value pair. The relationships are stored as the Relationship name (e.g., NextSegment) followed by the list of nodes that have this relationship (e.g., ThisNode, Node2).

Composite node: The entry for a composite node is similar to that of a segment, except that it contains a Child List instead of a Segment Boundaries field. The Child List is a

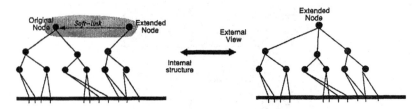

Figure 7.   Extension of a node.

list of the nodes that are descendents of this composite node in the annotation subgraph
structure.

Extended node: An extended node is a special type of a composite node. The structure
of a node can only be changed by the owner viewgroup. However, other viewgroups,
when given *extend* permission, can extend the structure of a node by using a soft-links.
An extended node has a unique field called *original node* which points the original node
from which the current node is extended (see figure 7).

The viewgroup table maintains one entry for each viewgroup that contains points to the
list of its members and their permissions as well as the list of the root nodes accessible to the
viewgroup. Any browsing and/or modification operations by the members of a viewgroup
is started from this viewgroup table entry.

3.2.   Operations on hierarchy

The operations on the nodes in the annotation hierarchy are:

- Creation/deletion of a node
- Extension of a node
- Insertion/deletion of annotations
- Query using the hierarchy

as well as

- Creation/deletion/maintenance of membership list of a viewgroup
- Insertion/deletion of viewgroups to current viewgroup list

Insertion/deletion of a node can be only done by the owner viewgroup. When a new
segment or composite (or extended) node is created, it is inserted into the Node Table, with
the various fields in the entry initialized to appropriate values. Once a node is created, the
owner can define the viewgroups and their permissions to the node.

3.3. *Composition of objects via query*

A query can be used to prune a subtree(s) rooted at a selected node(s). The query specifies the component objects and sub-objects to be selected based on the annotations and structural relationships used to identify these components. The query language is based on Boolean combinations of simple predicates [16] that test for identifying annotation attributes or relations. As in video algebra, the query operates by recursively examining every sub-node in the selected tree. Selected nodes results in a pruned subtree where only the matched nodes and its ancestors (but not siblings) are retained. The selected and pruned subtree can be made persistent by including it in the hierarchy forest. At each stage, only those attributes and relationships are considered that are visible to the viewgroups to which the user belongs. As explained earlier, the user can further select the scope of a search in the query by specifying a list of viewgroups.

Attribute synonym matching.   Without attribute synonym matching, a query searching for selected nodes with a particular attribute will not select nodes annotated with synonym for that attribute. Synonyms include not only a different word with the same meaning, but also different forms of the same word (singular vs. plural, noun vs. verb, etc.) and expressions (e.g., employer vs. employed by). *Attribute synonym matching* selects nodes not only with exact attribute matches, but also with synonym matches. For example, the marketing group may have an attribute named "team" in its annotation while the scheduling group (or a query) may have an attribute "department". Currently, BRAHMA uses a synonym dictionary (customizable by users) for attribute synonym matching.

4. Playback and media delivery

The playback of a composite media object or a simple physical segment will result in retrieval of its component media objects. The media objects are large and can not be easily transported from client to client. In most environments, the content (e.g., video) data would not be replicated, rather would be stored in centralized server sites (e.g., video server) as shown in figure 1. To avoid jitter the content of the entire media object can be downloaded to the display site. This would incur a substantial storage overhead and/or latency in start up. Alternatively, the data can be delivered isochronously over a bandwidth guaranteed channel [4]. Note that for presentation of composite media objects all the data streams for component objects need to be delivered isochronously [15]. The structural information maintained in BRAHMA can be used to intelligently prefetch and/or to cache content at the client for reuse [9, 15].

Multimedia presentation inherently requires huge amounts of data, and thus, large amounts of system resources along the data paths need to be reserved. Furthermore, several media objects could be presented in parallel over some period of time during the presentation of a composite multimedia object, requiring a lot more resources at the same time instant. Therefore, careful resource reservation and allocation schemes are necessary to improve the system throughput. Below we show how structural information can help increase the efficient retrieval and delivery of media data.

4.1. JINSIL delivery subsystem

The resource reservation and object delivery at each stage of data delivery path is handled by a separate layer called JINSIL [15]. At each stage, JINSIL considers the available resources (BW and buffer) and uses advance reservation, prefetching and reordering of presentation structure (when allowed) to minimize latency and/or improve resource utilization.

Figures 8 and 9 show the interactions of JINSIL with the client and the server component. Upon receiving a presentation request from an user, the *composite media player* invokes JINSIL to test the feasibility of the presentation under the client buffer size and the bandwidth limitation. If feasible, an *object delivery schedule* is constructed which will be used for playback. The objects may reside at remote sites and hence, resources need to be reserved in each component on the data path. The JINSIL layer in each stage (e.g., client, network, server) will pass an object delivery schedule to the next stage, that will in turn be used by that stage to reserve appropriate resources and to generate a prefetch schedule. The object delivery schedule of a stage is the prefetch schedule of the previous stage.

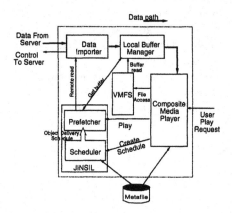

Figure 8.   JINSIL interactions in the client system.

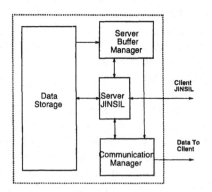

Figure 9.   JINSIL interactions in the server system.

Once the process of reservation and creation of object delivery schedules are successful, the composite media player starts playing back the presentation. The composite media player merely informs JINSIL (to start prefetching if in pull mode[1]) and starts accessing the virtual media file system (VMFS). The data importer (in pull mode) prefetches data in the filesystem buffer.

4.1.1. Advance reservation. As mentioned above, the presentation of a composite multimedia object which involves both parallel and sequential playback of media objects results in a time variable data delivery request. In a shared system, the availability of resources such as bandwidth and buffer space also varies with time. One simple resource allocation policy for variable bandwidth requirement is to reserve the maximum bandwidth between the client and server in each component. However, there are several disadvantages to this simple approach. First, in many commercial environments (e.g., cable or phone connection to home) the bandwidth is limited at the final stage of the network. This is referred to as the "Last Mile Problem". Presentation of complex media objects may require multiple streams of video, audio, image or text data for a short duration. Higher up on the data delivery paths the bandwidth may be shared across multiple presentations. Allocating the peak bandwidth reduces the number of presentations that can be admitted.

For the efficient retrieval of media data and for maximizing the utilization of system resources, JINSIL takes into account the true bandwidth requirement of the presentation. In many cases, this true bandwidth requirement is time-dependent (fluctuates with time). Note that in a shared environment, the availability of the system resources in general could be time dependent. Therefore, the resource reservation in JINSIL also reflects this time dependent availability of the resources.

4.1.2. Prefetching. When some buffer space becomes available in a system component, the JINSIL subsystem reshapes the bandwidth requirement and generates a prefetching schedule. Prefetching is motivated by the following three objectives.

- *Presentation satisfiability:* Prefetching makes it possible to satisfy certain presentation requests that cannot be satisfied otherwise due to high instantaneous demands for resources exceeding their availability.
- *Minimize peak bandwidth:* The prefetching scheme tries not only to satisfy the unsatisfiable data request, but also to further minimize the peak value in the reshaped data requirement. This will stabilize the availability of the shared system resources and thereby increase the admissibility of later requests to the system. Note that prefetching with minimum peak bandwidth is done in all (shared or dedicated) system components on the end-to-end data path, resulting in successive smoothing of BW requirements over all the components. Even when enough resources are available (as in a dedicated system component, e.g., the client system), reshaping of data requests still leads to less fluctuations in available resources in the server.
- *Load balancing:* Multimedia objects are often retrieved from different sources. For example, the server storage may be composed of multiple independent devices with separate bandwidths. In such cases, the data path for a presentation of composite multimedia object is partitioned into multiple sub-paths at some stages in the end-to-end delivery.

JINSIL considers the loads on different data paths and tries to reduce possible load imbalance between the data paths by trading off bandwidth and buffer space.

4.1.3. Utilizing flexibilities in presentation request.
In many cases, the specification of presentation request could be loosely structured. The temporal relationship across component media objects could be flexibly represented using minimum and maximum bounds. In this case, the schedule for object delivery can be adjusted within the allowed flexibility, depending on the availability of the system resources [2, 7]. In other cases, a user may request a set of media objects without specifying the presentation order among them. For example, a user may ask to retrieve all segments containing songs by a specific singer without specifying a presentation order. JINSIL can then arrange the presentation order and hence, the resulting retrieval order to maximize the system throughput [12].

4.2. Caching

The efficiency of data delivery and resource utilization are further improved by Generalized Interval Caching (GIC) policy [3]. Figure 10 illustrates the operation of the GIC policy. A presentation request from a user in the system may request retrieval of a long video sequence or it may be composed of requests for multiple short media objects, possibly chosen interactively. An interval is defined as the running segment between successive active requests for the same video object. In Movie 1 and Movie 2, several intervals are shown. For the requests to large video objects, GIC caches only small intervals between successive requests to a video sequence. The pages brought in by a preceding request are retained in the cache for reuse by a following stream. After reuse the pages are discarded immediately if the next following request is not served from the cache.

For interactive workloads consisting of small video objects, concurrent accesses are unlikely. A *predictive interval* is defined as the time between successive accesses to the same object (See, Clip 3 and Clip 4, in the figure). GIC still caches the shortest intervals whether the interval encompasses the entire video object or just a segment as in the large video objects. This policy has shown to be superior to the policy of caching the hottest

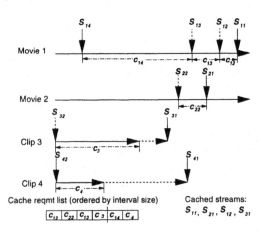

Figure 10. Illustration of Generalized Interval Caching.

movies. In addition, the policy dynamically adapts to the changing frequency of access to different movies unlike the static caching policy.

5. Conclusions

The large volume of data in multimedia databases makes it important to develop efficient methods for searching and retrieving information from such databases. Pure content-based browsing based on online analysis of the video content is limited by the high computational overhead incurred. Additionally, automatic extraction of high-level features (e.g., recognition of a specific person such as Clinton) is difficult. Manual annotation can be used to expand the scope of information associated with the video. However, even manual annotation cannot capture all the details associated with a video segment. Hence, it is necessary to allow each user to annotate the video with the information that is important to that user, and to allow this information to be shared with other users.

In this paper, we propose the BRAHMA system for efficient support of such applications. BRAHMA allows users to dynamically create and annotate a structured view of the videos, as well as share the structure and annotations with other users. For structuring the video, users may organize video segments into hierarchies that represent their view of the video. Each level of the hierarchy can be annotated with an *Attribute-value* pair, providing a richer scheme than a flat annotation structure. Note that in BRAHMA, the attributes that may be associated with the annotations are not pre-defined. The annotation hierarchy may be browsed or queried to locate particular video segments of interest. For efficient retrieval and delivery of the video BRAHMA uses pre-fetching, advance reservation and re-ordering of video segments.

Note

1. The data delivery model could be in pull or push mode. The difference between the two mode is that between any two stages, the object delivery schedule is used either by the source to deliver or by the destination to prefetch.

References

1. J. Allen, "Maintaining knowledge about temporal intervals," CACM, Vol. 26, No. 11, 1983.
2. K.S. Candan, B. Prabhakaran, and V.S. Subrahmanian, "Retrieval schedules based on resource availability and flexible presentation specifications," Technical Report, University of Maryland, 1996.
3. A. Dan and D. Sitaram, "Generalized interval caching policy for mixed interactive and long video environments," Multimedia Computing and Networking, Jan. 1996.
4. A. Dan, D. Sitaram, and P. Shahabuddin, "Dynamic batching policies for an on-demand video server," ACM Multimedia Systems, 1996.
5. A. Hampapur and H. Harashima, "Production model based digital video segmentation," Multimedia Tools and Applications, Vol. 1, pp. 9–46, March 1995.
6. R. Hjelsvold and R. Midstraum, "Modelling and querying video data," in Proceedings of VLDB Conference, 1994, pp. 686–694.
7. M. Kim and J. Song, "Multimedia documents with elastic time," in ACM Multimedia Conference'95, 1995.
8. M. Kim and J. Song, "Hyperstories: Combining time, space, and asynchrony in multimedia documents," Technical Report, IBM, RC 19277, 1995.
9. T.D.C. Little and A. Ghafoor, "Multimedia synchronization protocols for broadband integrated services," IEEE JSAC, Vol. 9, No. 9, pp. 1368–1382, Dec. 1991.

10. S. Marcus and V.S. Subrahmanian, "Foundations of multimedia database systems," Journal of ACM, Vol. 43, No. 3, pp. 474–523, May 1996.
11. A. Nagasaka and Y. Tanaka, "Automatic video indexing and full-motion search for object appearance," in IFIP TC2/WG2.6 Second Working Conference on Visual Database Systems, Sept. 1991, pp. 113–127.
12. R.T. Ng and P. Shum, "Optimal clip ordering for news on-demand queries," in 2nd International Workhop on Multimedia Information Systems, Sept. 1996, pp. 1–5.
13. K. Otsuji, Y. Tonomura, and Y. Ohba, "Video browsing using brightness data," Visual Communications and Image Processing, pp. 980–989, 1991.
14. R.A. Rowe, J.S. Boreczky, and C.A. Eads, "Indexes for user access to large video databases," in Storage and Retrieval for Image and Video Databases II, Symposium on Elec. Imaging Sci. and Tech., Feb. 1994.
15. J. Song, A. Dan, and D. Sitaram, "Jinsil: A system for presentation of composite multimedia objects in a distributed environment," IBM T.J. Watson Research Center, Computer Science Research Report RC 20476, June 1996.
16. R. Weiss, A. Duda, and D.K. Gifford, "Composition and search with a video algebra," IEEE Multimedia, pp. 12–25, Spring 1995.
17. B.L. Yeo, "Efficient processing of compressed images and video," Ph.D. Thesis, Princeton University, 1996.
18. H. Zhang, A. Kankanhalli, and S.W. Smoliar, "Automatic partitioning of full motion video," Multimedia Systems Journal, Vol. 1, pp. 10–28, July 1993.

Asit Dan received the B. Tech. degree in Computer Science and Engineering from the Indian Institute of Technology, Kharagpur, India, and the M.S. and Ph.D. degrees from the University of Massachusetts, Amherst, in Computer Science and Computer Engineering, respectively. His doctoral dissertation on "Performance Analysis of Data Sharing Environments" received an Honorable Mention in the 1991 ACM Doctoral Dissertation Competition and was subsequently published by the MIT Press.

Since 1990 he has been a Research Staff Member at the IBM T.J. Watson Research Center, Yorktown Heights, NY. He has published extensively on the design and analysis of video servers as well as transaction-processing architectures, and is a major contributor to various IBM products in the above areas. He holds several top-rated patents, and has received two IBM Outstanding Innovation Awards, and five IBM Invention Achievement Awards. Currently he is leading a project on the development of COYOTE middleware for supporting long-running transactional applications across autonomous business organizations.

Dr. Dan has served on various program committees, served as the tutorial chair for SIGMETRICS'97 and is currently serving as a guest editor for the IBM Journal of Research and Development.

Dinkar Sitaram is currently a Research Staff Member at the IBM T.J. Watson Research Center, Yorktown Heights, NY. He received the B. Tech. degree in ECE from Indian Institute of Technology, Kharagpur, the M.S. and Ph.D. degrees in Computer Sc. from the University of Wisconsin-Madison.

Dr. Sitaram has published extensively on multimedia servers, including book chapter, Outstannding paper and invited papers. He has worked jointly with Dr. Dan on the design and development of video servers on various IBM platforms. The work in these areas culminated in several top rated patents. He has received IBM Outstanding Innovation Award and various Invention Achievement Award for this work.

His current research interests include Internet based multimedia applications and transaction processing. Dr. Sitaram is currently serving on the editorial board of the Journal of High Speed Networks.

Junehwa Song is a research staff member at IBM T.J. Watson Research Center. He received his Ph.D. from the Department of Computer Science, University of Maryland at College Park in 1997, his M.S. from State University of New York at Stony Brook 1990, and his B.S. from Seoul National University, Seoul Korea in 1988.

He has been working on various issues in the distributed multimedia systems and compressed video processing. He has been awarded an IBM Cooperative Fellowship from 1995 to 1997.

Multimedia Tools and Applications 7, 103–132 (1998)

Handling Updates and Crashes in VoD Systems

EENJUN HWANG   hwang@cs.umd.edu
KEMAL KILIC   kemal@cs.umd.edu
V.S. SUBRAHMANIAN   vs@cs.umd.edu
Department of Computer Science, University of Maryland, College Park, MD 20742

Abstract.   Though there have been several recent efforts to develop disk based video servers, these approaches have all ignored the topic of updates and disk server crashes. In this paper, we present a *priority based model* for building video servers that handle two classes of events: *user* events that could include enter, play, pause, rewind, fast-forward, exit, as well as *system* events such as insert, delete, server-down, server-up that correspond to uploading new movie blocks onto the disk(s), eliminating existing blocks from the disk(s), and/or experiencing a disk server crash. We will present algorithms to handle such events. Our algorithms are provably correct, and computable in polynomial time. Furthermore, we guarantee that under certain reasonable conditions, continuing clients experience jitter free presentations. We further justify the efficiency of our techniques with a prototype implementation and experimental results.

Keywords: video server, updates, disk crashes, constraints, priority and optimal handling

1. Introduction

Over the last few years, there has been a tremendous drop in digitization costs, accompanied by a concomitant drop in prices of secondary and tertiary storage facilities, and advances in sophisticated compression technology. These three advances, amongst others, have caused a great increase in the quality and quantity of research into the design of video servers [2, 4, 6, 10, 11, 16].

Most models of video servers to date assume the following parameters:

1. Movies are stored, in part, or in their entirety, on one or more disks.
2. The video-on-demand VoD system is responsible for handling "events" that occur. Client events that have been studied include:

   - the enter of a new client into the system, requesting a movie,
   - the exit of an existing client from the system.
   - the activities of continuing clients (e.g., play, fast forward, rewind, pause).

   "Handling" an event refers to the process by which the VoD server assigns jobs to different disk servers, so as to optimize some performance criterion. A variety of algorithms to "handle" the above events have been studied by researchers.

All the above events are "user" events, in the sense that they are invoked or caused by the activities of a user of the VoD system. However, in reality, there is another class of events

that must be accounted for, which we call *system events*, which includes events such as
server-down (specifying that a certain disk server has crashed), server-up (specifying
that a disk server that had previously crashed is "up" again), insert (specifying that the
system manager wishes to include some new movies (or blocks of movies) on a disk),
and delete (specifying that the system manager wishes to delete some movies from a
server's disk array). Most work to date on server crashes has focused on the important
topic of *recovery* of data on the crashed disk, but has not really looked into how to satisfy
clients in the VoD system who were promised service based, in part, on the expectation that
the crashed disk would satisfy some requests. The main focus of this paper is to develop
VoD server algorithms that can handle not just user events, but can also handle system
events.

The problem of *updates* in video servers is crucial for several applications where video
data is being gathered at regular intervals and being placed on the VoD system. For example,
a movie-on-demand vendor may, at regular intervals, include new movies in the repertoire of
movies offered to potential customers. These movies need to be placed on the disk array that
the vendor may be using, leading to an insert operation. Similarly, in news-on-demand
systems, new news videos and audio reports may become available on a continuing basis,
and these need to be made available to editors of news programs for creating their current and
up to date news shows. In many similar systems today, this is done by taking the system
"down", accomplishing the update, and then bringing the system back "up" again. The
obvious undesirable aspect of this way of handling updates is that service must be denied
to customers who wish to access the server when it is down, thus leading to lost revenues
for the VoD vendor. The algorithms proposed in this paper treat updates as (collections of)
events, and schedule them to occur concurrently with user-events in a manner that ensures
that:

1. existing customers see no deterioration (under some reasonable restrictions) in the quality
   of service, and
2. the update gets incorporated in a timely fashion. In particular, our algorithms will flexibly
   adapt to the load on the disks, so as to incorporate as much of the update as possible
   when resources are available, and to reduce the update rate when resources have been
   previously committed.
3. the system is not "taken down" in order to accomplish the update.

Unlike the issue of updates, disk crashes have certainly been studied extensively over
the years [2, 12]. However, consider the problem of a VoD server that has made certain
commitments to customers. When a crash occurs, the VoD server must try to ensure that
any client being serviced by the disk that crashed be "switched" to another disk that can
service that client's needs. Furthermore, the VoD server must ensure that the fact disk d
has crashed be taken into account when processing new events. In the same vein, when
a disk server that had previously crashed comes back "up", this means that new system
resources are available, thus enabling the VoD server to take appropriate actions (e.g.,
admit waiting clients, re-distribute the load on servers to achieve good load balance, etc.).
We show how our framework for handling updates can handle such crashes as well (under
certain limitations of course).

In particular, we propose an algorithm called the VSUC ("Video Server with Updates and Crashes") algorithm, that handles events (including user events, as well as update events and crashes) and has several nice properties. In particular:

- VSUC guarantees that under certain conditions, it ensures continuous, jitter free service for clients, once they have been admitted. (We will make the conditions precise in Theorem 4.1).
- VSUC also guarantees (again under certain conditions), that no client is denied service for arbitrarily long (cf., Theorem 4.2).
- VSUC reacts to client events, as well as system events in polynomial time.

2. System architecture

Throughout this paper, we will use the term *video block* (or just *block*) to denote a video segment. We will assume that the size of a block is arbitrary, but fixed. In other words, one VoD application may choose a block to be of size 30 frames, while another may consider it to be of size 60 frames. As our video data is stored on disk, this means that the start of each *video block* is located on a single page of any disk that contains the block.

As data is laid out on a collection of disks, we will assume that this collection of disks is partitioned into disjoint subsets $DC_1, \ldots, DC_n$. We will furthermore assume that all disks in DC_i are homogeneous (i.e., have identical characteristics) and a single disk server DS_i regulates access to the disk drives in DC_i. It is entirely possible that DC_i contains only one disk, but it could contain more. Note that there is no requirement that two disk collections DC_i, DC_j need to have the same characteristics and hence, disks in DC_i may have vastly different characteristics than those in DC_j—this is what accomplishes heterogeneity.

The design of disk servers is now well known [2, 4, 6, 10, 11, 16]. In its simplest form, a disk server is a piece of software that, given a physical disk address, retrieves the object located at that address. In our case, disk servers DS_i mediate access to a collection DC_i of disks, which means that given a disk-id and a physical disk address, the server retrieves the block located at the given disk address on the specified disk. Figure 1 shows the structure of the system as described informally above.

In our architecture, the video server is responsible for the following tasks:

1. When an event (user event or system event) occurs, the video server must determine how to handle the event. This is accompanied by creating a schedule to accomplish the event, and deciding what instructions must be sent to the disk server(s) involved to successfully handle the event. For example, for a user event play, such instructions could include: Fetch (for client cl_id) the block starting on page p of disk d. Note that the disk server does not necessarily need to know the client's identity, cl_id.
2. In addition, the video server may need to "switch" clients from one disk server to another. For example, client cl_id_1 may be being served by disk server DS_1. If a new client cl_id_{20} requests a movie (or block) that is only available through disk server DS_1 and if disk server DS_1 is already functioning at peak capacity, then it may be possible to "switch" client cl_id_1 to another disk server (say DS_2) if disk server DS_2 has the needed to satisfy client cl_id_1.

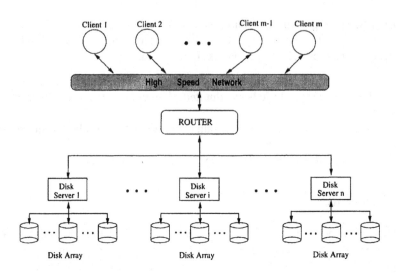

Figure 1.   System structure.

3. Third, the video server may "split" a job into smaller, manageable jobs, and distribute these smaller jobs to different servers, which leads to better system utilization.

4. Fourth, whenever events such as disk server crashes occur, the VoD server must re-assign the existing clients to other servers (when possible) and schedule *system generated recovery events* so as to minimize the damage caused by the crash.

2.1.   System parameters

In any VoD system, the participating entities may be divided into the following components:

1. Servers: these are the disk servers that retrieve specified blocks from the relevant disks;
2. Clients: these are the processes that are making/issuing requests to the servers; and
3. Data: this includes the movie blocks laid out on the disks.

In order to successfully model a VoD system, and develop provably correct and efficient algorithms for this purpose, we must model each of the above parameters, as well as the interactions between the above components.

Figures 2, 3, and 4 show the notations we use to denote the relevant parameters of servers, clients, and movies, respectively.

Throughout this paper, we assume that there is a set $\mathcal{MOVIE} = \{\mathcal{M}_1, \ldots, \mathcal{M}_r\}$ of movies that we wish to store on disk. Each movie $\mathcal{M}_i$ has $\mathsf{bnum}(\mathcal{M}_i)$ "blocks". A block denotes the level of granularity at which we wish to store and reason about the media-data. For example, a block may be a single-frame (finest granularity) or a consecutive sequence of (100 frames). The application developer is free to select the size of a block in any way s/he wishes, but once such a block size is selected, s/he is committed to using the selected

Symbol	Meaning
buf(i, s)	The total buffer space associated with the disk server i at state s.
cyctime(i, s)	The total cycle time for read operation by the server i at state s.
dtr(i, s)	The total disk bandwidth associated with the disk server i at state s.
timealloc(i, j, s)	The time-slice allocated to client j at state s by server i.
$\mu_s(i)$	The set of servers handling request by client i at state s.
$\wp(\mathcal{M}_i, b, s)$	The set of severs that contain block b of movie $\mathcal{M}_i$ according to placement mapping $\wp$ at state s.
server_client(i, s)	The set of all clients that have been assigned a non-zero time-allocation by disk server i at state s.
server_status(i, s)	The status flag for server i. It is true when the server is working, false otherwise.
switchtime(i, s)	The time required for the disk server i to switch from one client's job to another client's job at state s.
bufreq(i, j, s)	The buffer space needed at the server i to match the consumption rate of client j at state s.
priority(e, s)	The priority of the event e at state s.

Figure 2. Server parameters.

Symbol	Meaning
cons(i, s)	The consumption rate of client i at state s.
data(i, j, s)	The set of data blocks that server i is providing to client j at state s.
inuse(i, s)	This set consists of 3-tuples, $(j, \mathcal{M}_k, b)$, it specifies that the server i is providing block b of movie $\mathcal{M}_k$, to client j at state s.
active_client(s)	The set of all clients that are active at state s.
movie_client(m, s)	The set of all clients that are watching movie m at state s.
rew_win(i, s)	The size of rewind window for client i at state s. This means the client can not rewind the movie more than that many blocks.
ff_win(i, s)	The size of fast forward window for client i at state s. This means the client can not fast forward the movie more than that many blocks.
play_win(i, s)	The time limit for client i to access the system at state s.
pause_win(i, s)	The time limit for client i to pause at state s.

Figure 3. Client parameters.

Symbol	Meaning
bnum$(\mathcal{M}_i)$	The number of blocks for a movie $\mathcal{M}_i$.

Figure 4. Movie parameters.

block size for the application. In other words, they are free to choose their block size as they wish, but once they make the choice, they must stick to it.

3. State transition model

In this paper, we will develop a *state transition* model that has the following properties:

- A *state* is any feasible configuration of the system, and includes information such as: which disk server(s) are serving a client, and what service they are providing to the client, and what resources are committed by the server to the client to accomplish the service provided.
- The state of the system may change with time, and is triggered by *events*. Events include:
  - Client events such as enter, exit, fast-forward, pause, rewind, play, as well as
  - Server events such as server-down, server-up where a server goes "down" or comes back "up", and
  - Manager events such as insert, delete. Note that manager events could either be initiated by a human VoD system manager, or by a tertiary storage device that is staging data onto disk (though we will not go into this possibility in detail in this paper).

3.1. What is a state?

A *system state s* consists of the following components:

1. A set active_client(s) of active clients at state s.
2. The current cyctime(i, s) of each server in the system.
3. The consumption rates of the active clients (cons(i, s)) at state s.
4. The time, timealloc(i, j, s), within cyctime(i, s) that has been allocated by server i to client j at state s.
5. The locations ($\wp(m, b, s)$) of each movie block, i.e., the set of all servers on which block b of movie m is located at state s.
6. The set of data blocks (data(i, j, s)) being provided by server i to client j at state s.
7. A client mapping μ_s which specifies, for each client C, a set of servers, $\mu_s(C)$, specifying which servers are serving client C.
8. A set down_servers(s) consisting of a set of servers that are down at state s.
9. A set insert_list(s) consisting of a set of 3-tuples of the form (i, m, b) where m is a movie, b is a block, and i is the server where this block will be inserted. (This set is used to model a set of insertion updates that are "yet to be handled.")
10. A set delete_list(s) consisting of a set of 3-tuples of the form (i, m, b) where m is a movie, b is a block, and i is the server where this block will be deleted. (This set is used to model a set of deletion updates that are "yet to be handled.")

A system state s must satisfy certain simple constraints that we list below.

1. *For each server i that is not down, the sum of the time-allocations assigned to the clients being served by that server must be less than the cycle time of the server.* This is captured by the expression:

$$(\forall i)\left(i \notin \texttt{down\_servers}(s) \rightarrow \left(\sum_{j} \texttt{timealloc}(i, j, s) \leq \texttt{cyctime}(i, s)\right)\right).$$

2. *If a server is processing a request for some data, then that data must be available in the server.* This is captured by the expression:

$$(\forall i)(\forall j)(m : [b1, b2] \in \texttt{data}(i, j, s) \rightarrow (\forall b)(b1 \leq b \leq b2 \rightarrow i \in \wp(m, b, s))).$$

3. *The sum of consumption rates of the clients being served by a given disk server must not exceed the total disk bandwidth of the server.* This is captured by the expression:

$$(\forall i)(\forall j)\left(\sum_{j:\texttt{timealloc}(i,j,s)>0} \texttt{cons}(j, s) \leq \texttt{dtr}(i, s)\right).$$

4. *For each server i that is down, there is no active client.* This is captured by the expression:

$$(\forall i)(i \in \texttt{down\_servers}(s) \rightarrow (\texttt{server\_client}(i, s) = \emptyset)).$$

The above constraints specify the basic constraints that tie together, the resources of the VoD disk server system, and the requirements of the clients.

3.2. Prioritized events

Informally speaking, an *event* is something that (potentially) causes the VoD system to make a transition from its current state to a "next" (or new) state. The study of the performance of disk servers for multimedia applications varies substantially, depending upon the space of events that are considered in the model. In our framework, the space of events that are allowed falls into two categories:

- **Client events:** `enter`, `exit`, `pause`, `play`, `fast-forward`, `rewind`;
- **System events:** `server-up`, `server-down`, `insert`, `delete`.

Each event has an associated integer called the *priority* of the event, and a set of attributes. For example, the event `server-up` has an attribute specifying which server is up. Thus, `server-up(2,s)` specifies that the event "server 2 is up" has occurred at state s. Likewise, the event `insert` has three attributes—a server id, movie id, and a block number—specifying the server to which the event is assigned, the movie identifier and the movie block identifier. For example, the event `insert(2,m1,b1)` specifies that block $b1$ of movie $m1$ is being inserted into server 2.

The priority of an event is chosen either by the importance of the event or by the inherent attributes of the event. For example, handling client event like `play` inherently implies delivering continuous data stream to the client. If the data stream is interrupted due to any reason, then the client may experience degradation in the quality of service. This degradation has to be avoided by choosing appropriate priority for `play` event. As an example of system event, we can consider `delete` event. In the case where enough disk space is not available to download hot movies, the system should be able to make space by deleting data blocks as soon as possible. To expedite data deletion, the event should be assigned high priority.

Before specifying how events are handled, we describe some concepts underlying our approach.

3.3. Modeling usage constraints

In any VoD system, the system administrator may wish to enforce some "usage" constraints. In this paper, we do not try to force constraints upon the system. However, we do make available to the system administrator, the ability to articulate and enforce certain types of constraints that s/he feels are desirable for her/his system.

- **Pause time constraint:** A pause time constraint associates, with each client c, an upper bound, $pause\_win(c, s)$, on the amount of time for which the client can "pause" the movie s/he is watching. For example, suppose $pause\_win$ (John Smith, s) = 25. This means that as far as the system is concerned, John Smith's pause time cannot exceed 25 time units at state s. If the pause window expires, then the resources allocated to him by the VoD system will be "taken back" to satisfy other users' requests.

   In general, when a client "pauses", the server(s) satisfying the client's request continues to "hold" the resources which were assigned by the system. Clearly, holding such resources for an indefinite period is not wise. The pause window specifies, for each client, an upper bound on the period of time for which the client can pause the movie.

- **Fast-forward/Rewind window constraint:** In addition to pause window constraint discussed above, each client c is associated with *fast-forward* and *rewind* window constraint which specifies an upper bound on the number of data blocks that the client can fast-forward or rewind, respectively. The fast-forward and rewind windows associated with client c at state s is specified by $ff\_win(c, s)$ and $rew\_win(c, s)$.

- **Play time constraint:** Finally, sometimes, it might be desirable to put a restriction on the time that a client can be serviced by the server for a request. This constraint can help to prevent valuable resources from being taken for a arbitrary long time by irresponsible usage. Also, by establishing the maximum time that a client can access the system for a request, every request will eventually be satisfied by the server.

   The total play time constraint for a client i is specified by $play\_win(i, s)$. For example, $play\_win$ (John Smith, s) = 180 says that John Smith has at most 180 time units to finish viewing the current movie.

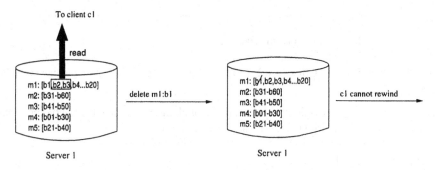

Figure 5. Deletion of a block.

3.4. Update boundaries

Suppose s is a system state (at some arbitrary point in time) and j is a client being served by a server i. The state s contains a data tuple specifying what data is being provided to the client by that server. For example, consider the situation where server 1 is presenting blocks $b2$ and $b3$ of movie $m1$ to client c_1.

Now, suppose the system administrator wishes to delete block $b1$ of movie $m1$ on server 1. Figure 5 shows this situation. While the system manager has the ability to make the request at any time, the precise time at which the request is actually scheduled (i.e., the precise time at which deletion of the block is scheduled) must take into account, the existing clients watching that movie w.r.t. the server in question. In this case, the question that needs to be addressed is: What happens if the client c_1 wishes to rewind to $b1$? If the deletion is incorporated immediately upon receipt of the deletion request, then the rewind request of the client will be denied—a situation that may or may not be desirable. Thus, at any given point in time, each client has an associated *rewind boundary* associated with each server, specifying "how far back" that server can support a rewind request issued by the client. The rewind boundary may change with time. *Rewind boundary*, and its dual concept, *fast-forward boundary*, are defined below.

Definition 3.1 (Rewind Boundary). The *rewind boundary* of a movie m w.r.t. server i in state s is defined as follows:

$$Rewind\_Boundary(m, s)$$
$$= \min\{b - \texttt{rew\_win}(j, s) \mid j \in \texttt{movie\_client}(m, s) \text{ and } (m, [b : b'])$$
$$\subset \cup_k \texttt{data}(k, j, s)\}$$

If the above set over which the min is performed is empty, that is, $\texttt{movie\_client}(m, s)$ is empty, then $Rewind\_Boundary(i, m, s) = \texttt{bnum}(m)$.

For example, let us return to the movie $m2$ at server 2 and the state s in which:

1. client c_5 is reading block $b4$ of movie $m2$;
2. client c_6 is reading block $b3$ of movie $m2$;
3. no other client is reading movie $m2$ (exactly what they are doing is not pertinent for this example).

If the rewind window for client $c5$ is 2, and that of client c_6 is 1, then the rewind boundary associated with server 2, movie $m2$ and state s is given by

$$\min(4 - 2, 3 - 1) = 2.$$

Let us try to see why this is the case, and what this statement means. (Figure 6 illustrates this reasoning).

- Two clients, viz. c_5, c_6, are reading (parts of) movie $m2$ from disk server 2. If we try to update the copy of movie $m2$ residing on disk server 2, the only clients who can be affected (in the current state) are therefore clients c_5 and c_6.
- Client c_5 is currently reading block $b4$ and his rewind window is of length 2, which means he can only go "back" 2 blocks in the movie by executing a rewind command. Effectively, this means that he cannot access any blocks before block $b2$.
- Likewise, client c_6 is currently reading block $b3$ and his rewind window is of length 1, which means he can only go "back" 1 block in the movie by executing a rewind command. Effectively, this means that he cannot access any blocks before block $b2$.

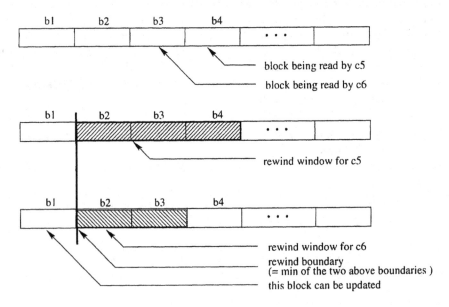

Figure 6. Rewind boundary computation.

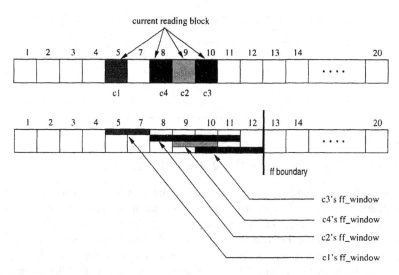

Figure 7. Fast forward boundary computation.

- As the minimum of these two blocks is $b2$, this means that neither client has read access to block $b1$ in this state.
- Thus, if we wish to update block 1 which lies "below" this rewind boundary, then this is "safe."

An analogous situation occurs w.r.t. *fast forward boundaries* which are defined as stated below.

Definition 3.2 (Fast Forward Boundary). The *fast forward boundary* of a movie m in state s is defined as follows:

$$FF\_Boundary(m, s)$$
$$= \max\{b + \texttt{ff\_win}(j, s) \mid j \in \texttt{movie\_client}(m, s) \text{ and } (m, [b : b'])$$
$$\subset \cup_k \texttt{data}(k, j, s)\}$$

If the above set over which the max is performed is empty, that is, $\texttt{movie\_client}(m, s)$ is empty, then $FF\_Boundary(m, s) = 0$.

For example, consider the single disk server in figure 7. This disk server, i, contains several movies, but only one of these, viz. movie $m4$ is shown in the figure. Blocks 1–5, 7–20 of this movie are available on the disk server i. Suppose that in state s, we have four clients watching this particular movie (other clients may be watching other movies) and that the blocks these clients are watching and the fast forward windows of these clients are as follows:

Client	Block being watched	ff_win
c_1	5	2
c_2	9	1
c_3	10	2
c_4	8	3

Then, the fast forward boundary is given by:

$$FF\_Boundary(i, m4, s) = \max\{5 + 2, 9 + 1, 10 + 2, 8 + 3\} = 12.$$

This means that only blocks 13–20 of the movie may be updated at this point of time.

The primary use of rewind boundaries and fast forward boundaries is to ensure that when an update request is made by the system manager, that the users viewing the application have the flexibility to rewind or fast forward, within the limits of their fast forward/rewind boundaries. Notice that it is not always possible to guarantee this. For example, in figure 7, if client c_1 wishes to fast forward to block 6, there is no way to satisfy this request without switching him to another disk server, because the disk server in figure 7 does not have block 6.

With these definitions in mind, we are now ready to define how to handle events.

4. Handling events

In this section, we provide detailed algorithms for handling events. We will first provide an abstract, declarative specification of *what* constitutes an appropriate way of handling events. Then, we will provide algorithms to successfully handle events.

4.1. Optimal event handling: Specification and semantics

Suppose s is a valid state of the system, and e is an event that occurs. In this section, we will first specify what it means for a state s' to handle the event e occurring in state s. This will be done without specifying how to find such a state s'. We will later provide algorithms to handle such events.

Definition 4.1 (Event handling). State s' is said to *handle* event e in state s iff one of the following conditions is true:

1. **New clients:** [$e =$ New client c enters with a request for movie m:]
   $(\exists i)(i \in \mu_{s'}(c) \wedge m : [1, 1] \in \mathtt{data}(i, c, s')$.
2. **Old clients:** [$e =$ Old client c exits the system]
   $\mu_{s'}(c) = \emptyset$.
3. **Continuing clients:**

   (a) ($e =$ Continuing client c watches, in "normal viewing" mode, block b of movie m)
   $(\exists i)(i \in \mu_{s'}(c) \wedge m : [b, b] \in \mathtt{data}(i, c, s'))$.

(b) $(e = \text{Continuing client } c \text{ pauses})$
   $(\exists i)(i \in \mu_{s'}(c) \wedge \text{data}(i, c, s') = \emptyset).$

(c) $(e = \text{Continuing client } c \text{ fast forwards from block } b \text{ to block } b + r \text{ where } r \leq$
   $\text{ff\_win}(c, s))$
   $(\exists i)(i \in \mu_{s'}(c) \wedge m : [b, \text{min}(\text{bnum}(m), b + r)] \in \text{data}(i, c, s')).$

(d) $(e = \text{Continuing client } c \text{ rewinds from block } b \text{ to block } b - r \text{ where } r \leq$
   $\text{rew\_win}(c, s))$
   $(\exists i)(i \in \mu_{s'}(c) \wedge m : [\text{max}(0, b - r), b] \in \text{data}(i, c, s')).$

4. **Server status event:**

(a) $(e = \text{disk server } i \text{ crashes})$
   $i \in \text{down\_servers}(s') \wedge \neg \, \text{server\_status}(i, s') \wedge (\forall c) i \notin \mu_s(c).$

(b) $(e = \text{disk server } i \text{ comes back "up"})$
   $i \notin \text{down\_servers}(s') \wedge \text{server\_status}(i, s').$

5. **Update event status:**

(a) $(e = \text{delete block } b \text{ of movie } m \text{ from server } i)$
   $i \notin \wp(m, b, s') \vee (i \in \wp(m, b, s') \wedge (i, m, b) \in \text{delete\_list}(s')).$

(b) $(e = \text{insert block } b \text{ of movie } m \text{ into server } i)$
   $i \in \wp(m, b, s') \vee (i \notin \wp(m, b, s') \wedge (i, m, b) \in \text{insert\_list}(s')).$

The handling of *update events* requires some intuition. Let us suppose, that we have a movie containing 100 blocks which is stored, in its entirety, on one disk server, and we have 2 clients c_1, c_2 who are watching the movie, via this server. Let us say that c_1 is watching block 45, and c_2 is watching block 50, and each of them is consuming 1 block per time unit (just to keep things simple). Let us further say that the system manager now wishes to update the entire movie, replacing old blocks by new ones (which may be viewed as a simultaneous insert and delete). Additionally, both clients c_1, c_2 have rewind windows and fast forward windows of 5 blocks each. Figure 8 shows this situation.

- At this stage, the rewind and fast forward boundaries for this movie are 40 and 55, respectively.

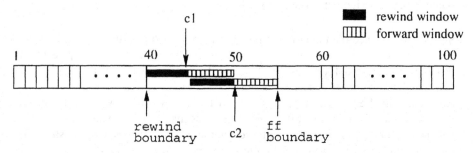

Figure 8. Example of deferred updates.

- This means that blocks $1, \ldots, 39$ and $56, \ldots, 100$ may be safely updated right away (assuming that enough bandwidth is available).
- The blocks b such that $40 \leq b \leq 55$ can only be updated later, i.e., the updating of these blocks must be *deferred*.
- For example, after one time unit, block 40 can be updated. After 2 time units, block 41 can be updated, and so on.

The skeptical reader will immediately wonder whether this definition allows us to postpone update events for an arbitrarily long time. The answer is that as stated above, update events could get deferred forever. To avoid this situation, and to also assign different priorities to different clients, we now introduce the notion of *priority*. Associated with each event (client initiated or system initiated, or deferred) is a priority. The higher the priority, the more important the event. In particular, if e is an update event, and e is deferred, then for each time unit that e is updated, we must "increment" e's priority by a factor δ_e. Thus, different events can have different associated "prioritization steps" which may be selected by the system manager, based on the importance of the event as determined by him/her. What this means is that the priority of an update events "gradually rises" till it can be deferred no longer. We discuss this scheme in detail below, and also show how the same idea applies to priorities on other (non-deferred) events.

4.2. Priority scheme for events

Whenever an event occurs, that event is assigned an initial priority, either by the system, or by the system administrator. The system maintains a list of default priority assignments. In the event of a different priority assignment being made by the system administrator, then the latter overrides the former.

Integers are used to represent "initial" priority assignments, though as we shall see, "non-initial" priority assignments may be real-valued. The precise integers used for initial priority assignment are not really important. What is more important is the *relative* priority ordering.

Default initial priority assignments. Figure 9 shows the initial priority assignments. The rationale for these assignments is discussed below.

1. System events have the highest priority. The reason for this is that a server crash, or a server coming "back up" are events that are hard to control. It is not possible, for instance, to defer or delay a crash. If it occurs, the system must transition to a new state that "handles" the crash as best as possible.
2. Next, existing clients already being served by the system must have the highest priority. The reason for this is that the VoD system has made a *commitment* to serve these clients well, and it must try to honor these commitments. However, each existing client may "spawn" different events, including `exit`, `pause`, `play`, `fast forward`, and `rewind`. Each of these events has a different priority.

Event Type	Event	Priority
System	Server_down	9
System	Server_up	9
Client (old)	Exit	7
Client (continuing)	Pause	6
Client (continuing)	Play	5
Client (continuing)	Fast-Forward	4
Client (continuing)	Rewind	4
Client (new)	Enter	3
Manager	Delete	2–7
Manager	Insert	1

Figure 9. Initial assigned priorities for different events.

(a) The highest priority is assigned to `exit` events. Processing an `exit` event early is desirable in general, because this can be done very fast, and furthermore, this frees up resources that may be used to satisfy other clients (continuing clients, as well as potential new clients).

(b) The next highest priority in this class is assigned to `pause` events because: first these events request no new resources (and hence, they can be satisfied immediately) and second, because of the `pause` window, these events may lead to future `exit` events that do in fact free up resources.

(c) The next highest priority in this class is assigned to `play` events. The reason for this is that in most cases, `play` events are relatively easy to satisfy as they merely require that the next block of the movie be fetched, and in most cases, the next block will be on the disk(s) that are already serving the client.

(d) The last two events in this category, with equal priority, are `rewind` and `fast forward`. These events may require substantial "switching" of clients (i.e., a client may be switched from its current server to another, because when blocks are skipped, the current server no longer has blocks that are several "jumps" ahead of the block currently being scanned.

3. New clients who just entered the system or have been waiting for service have the lowest priority among user events. The reason for this is that once the video server started to serve a client, that service should be continued with minimal disruption. But, in the case of new clients, it is reasonable to expect some delay before the service starts. However, this shouldn't cause new clients to wait infinitely. In this paper, this situation is handled by increasing the priority incrementally.

4. Of the system events, the `delete` event has the highest priority. The reason for this is that delete events can be accomplished by a very simple operation—just remove the pointers to the appropriate blocks. In contrast, `insert` events require greater resources (e.g., disk bandwidth is needed to write onto the disk).

113

Priority steps. Suppose an update request is received for block b of movie m in server i. Furthermore, suppose rwb and fwb denote, respectively, the rewind boundary, and the fast forward boundary associated with the current state. It is not difficult to see that we must have $rwb \le ffb$. The update cannot be carried out immediately if $rwb \le b \le ffb$. As a consequence, we might need to *defer* the update. However, as mentioned above, deferring the update might cause the event to be indefinitely delayed.

One possible way to avoid this is to assign higher priority to update events than client events, so that they can be handled first. The problem here is that this might cause the continuous streams to experience interruption. To handle update events eventually as well as to minimize their effect on continuous streams, we define *priority-step*. The priority step δ_u is specified by the system administrator for the update request u. δ_u is a non-negative real number, and its interpretation is as follows:

- Suppose s_0 is the current state (in which the update u occurs with the priority p shown in figure 9 (p must be either 1 or 2).
- Suppose $s_1, s_2, \ldots, s_k$ are states that occur, consecutively after s_0, all of which defer update u.
- Then the priority p_i of the update event u in state s_i is $(p + i \times \delta_u)$.

Thus, for example, suppose u is a deletion request, and the system manager assigns a step of 0.2 to u. Then, after 6 state changes (i.e., in state s_6), the priority of this update will be 3.2, which would exceed the priority of a new event (which is 3) occurring in that state. What this means is that if a new client enters the system in state s_6, and requests a movie, then the server in question would be asked to consider the higher priority update request u, as opposed to serving the customer.

By making the step size small, the system manager can allow a greater period of time to elapse before making the update have higher priority over new clients. For example, had the system manager set δ_u in the above example to 0.002, then 501 state changes would have to occur, before update u's priority exceeded that of a new client.

Furthermore, the system manager does not have to specify the same priority step for each update. Different updates can have different associated priorities, as would be expected in most real life systems.

We are now ready to give an algorithm that manipulates the priorities, such as those shown in figure 9, and the above priority steps, to handle events that occur at any given point in time.

Video server with updates and crashes (VSUC) algorithm

main **HandleEvents** (*NewEvents, OldEvents*)

```
{
    EvtList = sort events in NewEvents and OldEvents in decreasing order of priority ;
    WaitList = Ø ; /* set of events that can't be scheduled in this
      cycle */
    DoneList = Ø ; /* set of client events that have been scheduled
      successfully */
```

```
While ( !timeout and EvtList ≠ ∅ )
{
    evt = get the first event in EvtList ;
    switch ( evt.type )
    {
        case down :  handleServerDownEvents ( evt )
        case up :  handleServerUpEvents ( evt )
        case play, rewind, fast-forward :  handleContEvents ( evt )
        case pause :  handlePauseEvents ( evt )
        case exit :  handleExitEvents ( evt )
        case enter :  handleEnterEvents ( evt )
        case insert:  handleInsertEvents ( evt )
        case delete:  handleDeleteEvents ( evt )
    }
}

If ( EvtList ≠ ∅ )
    increase priority of each event in EvtList by δ_evt ;

OldEvents = merge events from EvtList and WaitList ;
return ( OldEvents ) ;
}
```

procedure **HandleServerDownEvents** (*evt*)
```
{
    for each data block b_i in crashed server do
        update placement mapping so that b_i is not visible ;

    for each event e_i in crashed server do
        insert e_i into EvtList preserving the sorted order ;
}
```

procedure **HandleServerUpEvents** (*evt*)
```
{
    for each data block b_i in recovered server do
        update placement mapping so that b_i is visible ;
}
```

procedure **HandleExitEvents** (*evt*)
```
{
    release resources and data structures allocated for evt ;
}
```

procedure **HandleContEvents** (*evt*)
{

    Blocks = set of blocks necessary for servicing *evt* ;

```
/* depending on event type, the way blocks are read from
   disks can be */
/* different. For example, in play event, certain number of
   continuous */
/* blocks should be read, but in rewind (ff) event, some inter-
   mediate blocks */
/* can be skipped to match the speed */
```

    if (servers that have been assigned to *evt* contain all blocks in *Blocks*)
    {

        update the data component of *evt* ;
        insert *evt* into *DoneList* ;
        return ;

    }
    DServers = set of servers that contain all blocks in *Blocks* ;
    if (*DServers* $= \emptyset$) /* placement mapping error */
    {

        /* make *evt* considered after block insertions */
        decrease *evt*'s priority by δ_{evt} ;
        insert *evt* into *EvtList* preserving the sorted order ;
        return ;

    }
    RServers = set of servers in *DServers* satisfying resource constraints ;
    if (*RServers* $= \emptyset$)
    {

        if (*evt*'s priority has been decreased previously)
        {

            Finished = **false** ;
            Svlist = *DServers* ;
            while (*Svlist* $\neq \emptyset$ and !*Finished*) do
            {

                s = select one server randomly from *Svlist* ;
                Svlist = *Svlist* - { *s* } ;
                Switchables = {*e* | event *e* is served by *s* and there exists *s'* ($\neq s$) that
                    satisfies *e* } ;
                while (*Switchables* $\neq \emptyset$ and !*Finished*) do
                {

                    e' = select one event randomly from *Switchables* ;
                    Switchables = *Switchables* - {*e'*} ;
                    if (*evt* can be served using the resources that will be released
                        from *e'*)

```
                {
                    release resources from e′ and update resource allocation of s ;
                    allocate resources to evt and update resource allocation of s ;
                    allocate resources to e′ and update resource allocation of s′ ;
                    put evt into DoneList ;
                    Finished = true ;
                }
            }
        }

        if ( !Finished )
        {
            /* make evt scheduled prior to other clients in next
               cycle; */
            increase evt's priority by δ′ₑᵥₜ ;
            insert evt into WaitList ;
        }
    } else
    {
        /* make evt considered after scheduling other normal
           continuing clients */
        decrease evt's priority by δ″ₑᵥₜ ;
        insert evt into EvtList preserving the sorted order ;
    }
} else
{
    MaxEval = - 1 ;
    for each server sᵢ in RServers do
    {
        Eval = evaluate sᵢ for the specified criteria ;
        if ( Eval > MaxEval )
        {
            MaxEval = Eval ;
            BestSv = sᵢ ;
        }
    }
    allocate resources to evt from BestSv ;
    update resource allocation of BestSv ;
    insert evt into DoneList ;
}
}

procedure HandlePauseEvents ( evt )
{
```

yield disk bandwidth to update events for next cycle ;
keep the other status unchanged ;
}

procedure **HandleEnterEvents** (*evt*)
{

```
/* enter event can be handled in a way similar to handling
   continuous events. */
/* The difference is that in the case of enter events,
   resources have not * /
/* been assigned previously. Therefore, checking if already
   assigned server */
/* can handle the event is not necessary for enter events. */
```

}

procedure **HandleInsertEvents** (*evt*)
{

s_{evt} = server that data block is inserted into ; `/* specified in` *evt* `*/`
$Dsize$ = the size of data that is inserted into s_{evt} ;
$Msize$ = maximum data size that server s_{evt} can handle using available resources ;
if ($Msize \geq Dsize$)
{
     allocate resources to *evt* ;
     update resource allocation of s_{evt} by $Dsize$;
     update placement mapping information of s_{evt} ;
} else
{
     /* $Dsize$ can't be inserted in its entirety */
     allocate resources to *evt* ;
     update resource allocation of s_{evt} by $Msize$;
     reduce *evt*'s data size by $Msize$;
     increase *evt*'s priority by δ_{evt} ;
     insert it into *WaitList* ;
}

}

procedure **HandleDeleteEvents** (*evt*)
{

b_{evt} = block number that is deleted ;
calculate the rewind and fast forward boundary of the movie ;
if (b_{evt} < **rewind_boundary** or b_{evt} > **ff_boundary**)
     delete b_{evt} and update placement mapping information ;
else

```
{
        /* evt is deferred to next cycle */
        increase evt's priority by δ_{evt} ;
        insert it into WaitList ;
}
}
```

It is easy to prove that the VSUC algorithm described above has a number of nice properties, as stated in the theorems below. An informal description of these properties is as follows:

- *Under certain reasonable conditions, clients who have already been admitted to the system experience no jitter, independently of what other events occur.* This result applies when (1) if the placement mapping is "full" (i.e., either the entire movie is available through a server, or none of it is), and (2) when the client watches a movie entirely in "normal" viewing mode, and (3) no server outages occur.
- *Every event eventually gets handled as long as servers that go "down" eventually come back "up."*
- *The VSUC algorithm runs in polynomial time, i.e., if the current state is s and if ev is the set of events that occur, then a new state s' (together perhaps with deferred events) is computed in polynomial time.*

Theorem 4.1 (Continuity of Commitments). *Suppose s is the current state of the system, and C_i is a continuing client in state s who is watching movie m in "normal" mode. Furthermore, suppose that:*
1. *movie m is contained in its entirety in each server sv $\in \mu_s(C_i)$ and*
2. *no server in $\mu_s(C_i)$ goes "down" at this time and*
3. *for all updates u (before client C_i entered the system,) that were deferred when client C_i enters, $pr_u \leq 5$ and $\delta_u \leq \delta_{C_i}$ where pr_u is the priority of the update u when client C_i enters the system, δ_u is the priority step associated with the update, and δ_{C_i} is the priority step associated with C_i.*
4. *for all updates u (before client C_i entered the system,) that enter the system after client C_i enters, $newpr_u \leq 5$ and $\delta_u \leq \delta_{C_i}$ where $newpr_u$ is the priority of the update u when it enters the system.*
Then client C_i's movie request event will be satisfied by the VSUC algorithm.

Proof Sketch: In the VSUC algorithm, the only event that diminishes the system's resources and that has a higher priority than a continuing client is a `server_down` event or a deferred update event. However, by the assumption in the statement of the theorem, no servers serving client C_i go down, and hence, the highest priority events are either deferred updates or continuing clients.

Suppose a server sv is serving client C_i's request (in part or in full). If no deferred events occur, then the same server can continue servicing client C_i's request for "next" blocks. However, if deferred events occur, then there are two possibilities:

1. Suppose the deferred update u was requested before client C_i entered the system. As $pr_u \leq 5$ and as $\delta_u \leq \delta_{C_i}$, it follows that throughout the normal playing of the movie, client C_i's priority is higher than that of the update u. Thus, server sv continues to serve client C_i without allowing deferred events to obtain priority over the client C_i.
2. On the other hand, if the deferred update was requested after client C_i entered the system, then client C_i is guaranteed to obtain priority over the update because $newpr_u \leq 5$ and $\delta_u \leq \delta_{C_i}$. Hence, client C_i can continue to be served by server sv.   □

The above theorem has important implications for **admission control**, both of new clients and of new updates.

- **Client admission:** To guarantee continuity of service, a new client C_i should be admitted to the system *only if* for all deferred updates u that need to be handled when client C_i enters the system, we must know that $pr_u \leq 5$ and $\delta_u \leq \delta_{C_i}$.
- **Update admission:** To guarantee continuity of service to existing clients, a new update u should be admitted to the system only if $newpr_u \leq 5$ and $\delta_u \leq \delta_{C_i}$.

Theorem 4.2 (All update events get handled eventually). *Suppose s is the current state of the system and ev is any update event that requires a set SV of servers. Further suppose that for all times $t >$ now and all servers in SV, if there exists a time $t' > t$ at which one or more servers in SV go down, then there exists a time $t^* > t'$ at which all servers in SV come back up. Then: for any update event ev that occurs now, there exists a time $t_{ev} \geq$ now such that ev gets handled at time t_{ev}.*

Proof Sketch: If update event ev does not get handled *now*, then, as $\delta_{ev} > 0$, in each execution of the VSUC algorithm, event ev's priority *strictly increases* till it exceeds 7, at which point t' in time, it will be handled unless one or more servers that are needed to service event ev are down. By the restriction in the statement of the theorem, there exists a time $t^* > t'$ at which all servers in SV are "up" simultaneously. We are guaranteed that this event will be handled latest at time t^*.   □

Theorem 4.3. *Suppose ev(t) is a set of events that occur at time t. The time taken for the the VSUC algorithm to terminate is polynomial in the sum of the number of events in ev(t) and the number of deferred events.*

Proof: It follows immediately that each function call in the main algorithm runs in time polynomial w.r.t. the above sum.   □

5. Experiments

5.1. Crash handling vs. survival rate

Simulation experiments of the suggested VoD architecture were carried out. As we mentioned above, the video server consists of multiple disk servers with possibly different relative performance characteristics. The performance characteristics of disk servers are

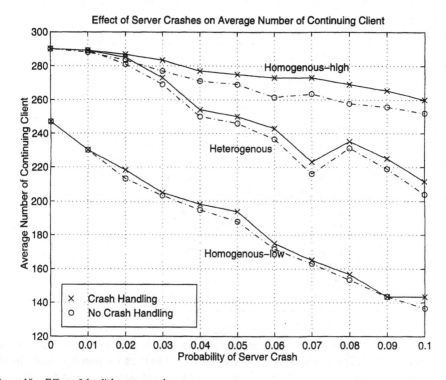

Figure 10. Effect of the disk server crashes.

defined from 1(the lowest) to 4 (the highest). Three disk server configurations considered in the experiments are homogeneous servers with highest performance characteristics, homogeneous servers with lowest performance characteristics, and heterogeneous servers with different performance characteristics [3].

In the following experiments, we examined the resilence of the video server against disk server crashes under different disk server configurations, i.e., how well the video server performs when crashes occur. The number of disk server crashes and crash time were generated randomly. We assumed that the crash recovery time is uniform. After the recovery time, the disk server would be available again for use. To compare the resilience of the video server, we repeated same experiment with different frequency of the server crashes, measuring average number of continuing clients after crashes.

Figure 10 shows the effect of handling server crashes on the number of continuing clients. Regardless of server configuration, the system could support more streams with crash handling than without crash handling. However, depending upon the performance characteristics of the servers involved, the number of continuing clients that could be supported varied. The most notable improvement was shown in the case of the homogeneous server with highest performance characteristics.

As the frequency of disk crashes increases, the system will experience much more difficulty scheduling clients because resources and video data at the crashed servers are not available during crash recovery.

Table 1.   Parameters used in simulation.

1	Number of video clips	800
	10 minutes video	400
	20 minutes video	200
	40 minutes video	100
	80 minutes video	100
2	Size of video segment	10–80 minutes
3	Size of block	0.2 seconds' compressed video data
4	Number of requests	800–2000
5	Request pattern	Based on actual data referenced in [5]
6	Number of disk servers	30
7	Types of disk servers	Buffer / Disk bandwidth
	Group 1	64MB / 32MB
	Group 2	48MB / 24MB
	Group 3	32MB / 16MB
	Group 4	16MB / 8MB
8	Buffer size	Avg. 50 MB per server
9	Disk bandwidth	Avg. 20 MB combined per server

To measure how many clients can continue even after server crashes, we define *survival rate* as the ratio of clients who can continue to be served to the total number of clients in the system when crash occurs. Figure 11 shows that homogeneous disk servers showed a stable survival rate with respect to disk crashes. However, heterogeneous disk servers showed a noticeable variation in the survival rate.

In the next experiment, we used different disk server configurations and examined the effect of crashes on disk servers with different performance characteristics. The request pattern for the video data is same as above. Table 1 shows several parameters related to the experiment.

For the experiment, we used four different types of disk servers. Servers with the highest performance characteristics belong to group 1 and servers with the lowest belong to group 4. Under normal operation, servers with higher performance characteristics store more video segments and support more concurrent streams than those with lower performance characteristics. Therefore, the effects of disk crashes will vary depending on the performance characteristics of the server that crashes.

Figures 12(a) to (d) show how many clients on the crashed server continue to be served even after disk crashes (under varying system load). For the comparison, we showed both the number of continuing clients with crash handling and without crash handling. Here, "after no crash handling" means that the streams on the crashed server(s) will be discontinued unconditionally.

In these figures, the difference between the top line and the bottom line is the number of clients on the crashed disk. On the average, our crash handling VoD server algorithm can

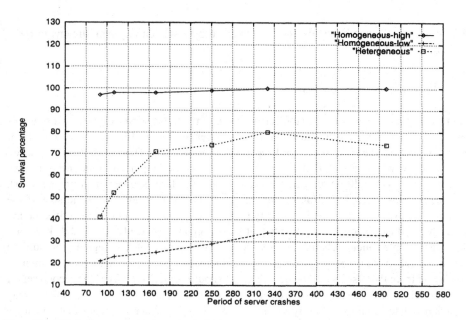

Figure 11. Effect of server crash rate on survival rate.

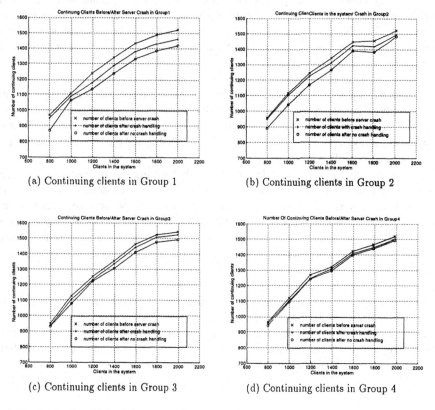

(a) Continuing clients in Group 1

(b) Continuing clients in Group 2

(c) Continuing clients in Group 3

(d) Continuing clients in Group 4

Figure 12. Continuing clients after server crash.

satisfy about half the clients affected by the crash by rescheduling their streams to other available servers.

5.2. *Performance vs. segmentation*

In this experiment, we examined the performance of the video server for different segmentations—here a segment refers to a continuous sequence of video blocks. We assumed that video objects are divided into several segments of equal size. These segments are placed in the disk servers in a way that adjacent segments should be placed in the different disk servers (otherwise multiple segments are merged into one large segment on a single server). Video segments were placed on the servers in a manner proportional to the size of the disk storage available, i.e., the probability that a video segment is placed on a disk having capacity 5 GB is 5 times the probability that same segment is placed on a 1 GB disk. Under this segment placement scheme, any two disk servers with adjacent segments should be synchronized for the seamless display of video stream. That is, as soon as a segment is consumed from the first server, the next segment should be delivered from the second server without delay. If the second server cannot deliver next segment in time, then clients may experience deterioration in quality of service. We will show later that this situation can be relaxed if we increase buffer space for each stream.

Figure 13(a) shows how many streams will experience intermediate stream delay due to server switches for retrieval of adjacent segments. When video objects are stored in their entirety, then there is no need for server switches for the ongoing streams. But, as the number of segments in a movie is increased, the number of clients experiencing intermediate delays due to server switch increases.

In figure 13(b), we examined average intermediate stream delay experienced by the clients. It shows that once video objects are segmented, the average stream delay decreases as the number of segments increases. This is due to the fact that with smaller segments, clients stay at the server for a shorter time than larger segments. With shorter stays at the servers, resource availability of disk servers become flexible and therefore server switching can be done more easily and frequently.

From figures 13(a) and (b), we might conclude that storing video objects in its entirety on one disk server is the best scheme. But two other criteria show that this scheme has some disadvantages as well. Figure 13(c) shows the server response time specifying how long each client has waited till the first frame of the video object was displayed. Under a moderate to a large number of clients in the system, the system response time increases sharply as the number of segments decreases. Also, the number of updates done during the simulation increases as the number of segments increases. Figure 13(d) shows how many update requests have been done during the simulation.

Furthermore, as mentioned earlier, intermediate stream delays due to server switches can be compensated to a certain degree if we increase buffer space for streams. From figure 13(b), average stream delay is less than 30 cycles when the total number of clients is 1800. Therefore, as we increase the buffer space for streams, the number of clients experiencing actual intermediate display delay will be reduced.

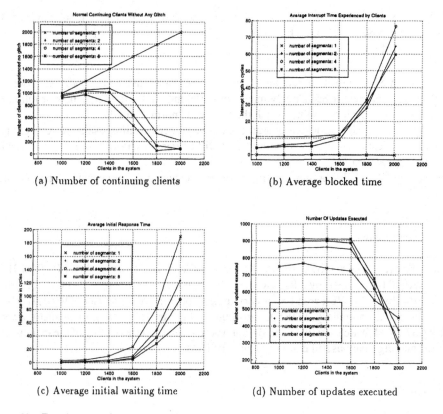

(a) Number of continuing clients

(b) Average blocked time

(c) Average initial waiting time

(d) Number of updates executed

Figure 13. Experiment results.

6. Conclusions

Though there has been extensive work on handling disk crashes most such work has occurred in the area of recovery of data on the crashed disk. Likewise, though there has been extensive work on developing systems support for handling VCR-like functions in video servers, this work has ignored two possibilities:

1. That during the operation of such a video server, *updates* might occur. The problem of handling such updates has not been adequately addressed in the literature.
2. Similarly, during the operation of such a video server, one or more servers might crash and/or otherwise become inaccessible. This means that any clients currently being served by those servers must be satisfied in some other way. To date, there has been no formal theoretical work on extending VoD servers to handle this possibility.

The primary aim of this paper is to provide a formal model of VoD systems that is capable of handling such events, as well as to provide the VSUC algorithm that can neatly handle the variations in resource availability that may arise as a consequence of such events. In particular, the VSUC algorithm has many nice properties that, to our knowledge, have been proposed for the first time.

- First, the VSUC algorithm guarantees that under certain reasonable conditions, users to whom the VoD server has already made commitments, will experience no disruption or jitter in service as long as they watch the movie in "normal" mode.
- Second, the VSUC algorithm guarantees (again under certain reasonable restrictions) that no request made by a continuing client will be denied service "forever", i.e., it will eventually be handled.
- Third, the VSUC algorithm reacts to both user events and system events, in polynomial time.

Acknowledgments

This work was supported by the Army Research Office under Grants DAAH-04-95-10174 and DAAH-04-96-10297, by ARPA/Rome Labs contract F30602-93-C-0241 (ARPA Order Nr. A716), by Army Research Laboratory under Cooperative Agreement DAAL01-96-2-0002 Federated Laboratory ATIRP Consortium and by an NSF Young Investigator award IRI-93-57756. We are grateful to Dr. B. Prabhakaran for a careful reading of the manuscript and for making many useful comments and critiques.

References

1. S. Berson and S. Ghandeharizadeh, "Staggered striping in multimedia information systems," in Proc. of ACM SIGMOD Conf. on Management of Data, Minneapolis, MN, 1994, pp. 79–90.
2. S. Berson, L. Golubchik, and R. Muntz, " Fault tolerant design of multimedia servers," in Proc. of ACM SIGMOD Conf. on Management of Data, San Jose, CA, 1995, pp. 364–375.
3. K.S. Candan, E. Hwang, and V.S. Subrahmanian, "An event-based model for continuous media data on heterogeneous disk servers," ACM Multimedia Systems Journal, accepted, to appear.
4. M.-S. Chen, D.D. Kandlur, and P.S. Yu, "Support for fully interactive playout in a disk-array-based video server," in Proc. ACM Multimedia, 1994, pp. 391–398.
5. A. Dan and D. Sitaram, "A generalized interval caching policy for mixed interactive and long video workloads," Multimedia Computing and Networking, San Jose, Jan. 1996.
6. A.L. Drapeau, D.A. Patterson, and R.H. Katz, "Toward workload characterization of video server and digital library application," in Proc. of ACM Sigmetrics Conference on Measurement and Modeling of Computer Systems, Nashville, May 1994.
7. C. Federighi and L. Rowe, "A distributed hierarchical storage manager for a video-on-demand system," in Proc. of the 2nd SPIE Symp. on Storage and Retrieval of Video Databases, 1994, pp. 185–197.
8. S. Ghandeharizadeh and C. Shahabi, "On multimedia repositories, personal computers, and hierarchical storage system," in Proc. of ACM Multimedia, 1994.
9. G. Miller, G. Baber, and M. Gillilana, "News-on-demand for multimedia networks," in Proc. of ACM Multimedia, 1993, pp. 383–392.
10. A.N. Mourad, "Issues in the design of a storage server for video-on-demand," ACM/Springer-Verlag Multimedia Systems, 1996.
11. A.L. Narasimha Reddy, "Scheduling and data distribution in a multiprocessor video server," in Proc. of IEEE Multimedia, 1995.

12. D. Patterson, G. Gibson, and R. Katz, "A case for redundant arrays of inexpensive disks," in Proc. of ACM SIGMOD Conf. on Management of Data, 1988.
13. C. Ruemmler and J. Wilkes, "An introduction to disk drive modeling," IEEE Computer, pp. 17–28, March 1994.
14. K. Salem and H. Garcia-Molina, "Disk striping," in Proc. of IEEE Conf. on Data Engineering, 1986.
15. J.L. Sharnowski, G.C. Gannod, and B.H.C. Cheng, "A distributed, multimedia environmental information system," in Proc. of IEEE Multimedia, 1995.
16. R. Tewari, R. Mukherjee, D.M. Dias, and H.M. Vin, "Design and performance tradeoffs in clustered video servers," in Proc. of IEEE-ICMCS, Tokyo, June 1996.
17. P. Venkat Rangan, H. Vin, and S. Ramanathan, "Designing and on-demand multimedia service," IEEE Communications Magazine, pp. 56–64, July 1992.
18. H. Vin, S.S. Rao, and P. Goyal, "Optimizing the placement of multimedia objects on disk arrays," in Proc. of IEEE Intl. Conf. on Multimedia Computing Systems, 1995, pp. 158–165.
19. B. Worthington, G. Granger, and Y. Patt, "Scheduling algorithms for modern disk drives," in Proc. of ACM SIGMETRICS Conference, 1994.

Eenjun Hwang received his B.S. and M.S. degrees in Computer Engineering from Seoul National University, Korea, in 1988 and 1990, respectively. Currently he is pursuing the Ph.D. degree in the Computer Science Department of the Unviersity of Maryland at College Park. He is currently working on distributed multimedia document presentation. His research interests include image and video retrieval, video server modeling and scheduling, and network protocol for multimedia document presentation.

Kemal Kilic received B.Sc. in 1994 from Bogazici University in Computer Engineering. He is currently an M.Sc. student in Computer Science at the University of Maryland, College Park. His research interests include multimedia, image processing.

V.S. Subrahmanian received his Ph.D. in Computer Science from Syracuse University in 1989. Since then, he has been on the faculty of the Computer Science Department at the University of Maryland, College Park, where he currently holds the rank of Associate Professor. He received the NSF Young Investigator Award in 1993 and the Distinguished Young Scientist Award from the Maryland Academy of Science in 1997. He has worked extensively in knowledge bases, bringing together techniques in artificial intelligence and databases. In particular, his work in the area of non-monotonic deductive databases where he proposed well received declarative semantics, as well as efficient implementation paradigms has been influential. He has also worked extensively in the handling of uncertainty in deductive databases, showing how fuzzy and probabilistic data may be neatly manipulated. Finally, he has worked extensively on multimedia systems, and made fundamental contributions to scalable implementation of such systems. More recently, he has been working on the problem of integrated heterogeneous data and software located across the Internet. He has proposed formal theoretical models for such integrations, as well as led the HERMES project for heterogeneous reasoning and mediator systems. Other implementation efforts he has led include multimedia projects such as MACS for media data, AVIS (for video data), and CHIMP for collaborative multimedia document presentation and authoring.

Prof. Subrahmanian has over 100 published/accepted papers, including ones in prestigious journals such as the Journal of the ACM, the ACM Trans. on Databases, IEEE Trans. on Knowledge and Data Engineering, Information and Computation, etc. He has edited two books, one on non-monotonic reasoning (MIT Press) and one on multimedia databases (Springer). He has co-authored an advanced database textbook (Morgan Kaufman, 1997), and is currently finishing a textbook on multimedia databases (Morgan Kaufman, Jan. 1998). He has given invited talks and served on invited panels at various conferences. In addition, he has served on the program committees of various conferences. He is on the editorial board of IEEE Transactions on Knowledge and Data Engineering and AI Communications. He serves on DARPA's Executive Advisory Council for the Advanced Logistics Program.

Multimedia Tools and Applications 7, 133–146 (1998)

A Resource Reservation Scheme for Synchronized Distributed Multimedia Sessions

WEI ZHAO   zw@cs.umd.edu
Mobile Computing and Multimedia Lab, Department of Computer Science, University of Maryland, College Park, MD 20742

SATISH K. TRIPATHI   tripathi@engr.ucr.edu
Bourns College of Engineering, University of California, Riverside, CA 92521

Abstract. Guarantees of services in a networked environment are provided by the proper allocation and scheduling of network and system resources. A lot of research in packet scheduling, QoS routing, traffic multiplexing, etc. has been aimed at providing deterministic or statistical service guarantees, while utilizing resources efficiently. In this paper, we propose a resource reservation scheme for a class of multimedia presentations. We characterize this class of multimedia presentations as synchronized distributed multimedia sessions, which we believe are important components of many multimedia applications. In addition to multimedia presentations, the reservation scheme applies to applications with synchronized resource requirements. Based on resource inquiry and interval analysis, the scheme is also able to find feasible resource allocation schedules for resource reservation requests. Built upon a layer of resource abstraction, the scheme suits well with today's heterogeneous network environment.

Keywords: resource reservation, multimedia presentation, synchronization, quality-of-service, advance reservation, bandwidth allocation

1. Introduction

Multimedia applications typically require some degree of quality of service (QoS) guarantees from the underlying networks and end-systems. For example, the remote playback of multimedia information such as video requires network services with given throughput, delay, delay jitter and loss guarantees, as well as end-system services to retrieve, process and display video frames that involves CPU, disk and buffer resources. Based on the QoS capability of the underlying network and end-system service they use, multimedia applications can be broadly classified into two categories. Applications assuming a deterministic service model rely on the exact provisioning of the negotiated service to perform satisfactorily; on the other hand, adaptive applications can adapt to resource fluctuations, at the cost of a possible degradation in perceptual quality. Though adaptive applications can perform well in some circumstances, there is always a bound on how much resource fluctuation that an adaptive application can tolerate while achieving acceptable quality. Therefore, even for adaptive applications, a certain degree of QoS guarantee is desirable.

Resource reservation seems to be a natural way to provide service guarantees in a finite resource environment. Explicit resource reservations allocate certain amount of resources (e.g., bandwidth) explicitly for each request, while implicit resource reservations use various forms of admission control policies to ensure that admitted requests obtain the specified services. In both cases, resources are reserved prior to their usage by the clients. Reserved resources are protected by resource managers who are obliged to fulfill the service guarantees.

Two mainstream resource reservation protocols, STII and RSVP, have been proposed in the Internet community [3, 5, 6, 12, 14]. RSVP is part of a broader proposal called Intergrated Services Packet Network (ISPN) by Internet Engineering Task Force (IETF) intended to establish a quality of service framework in the Internet [2, 4]. Both reservation protocols have similar mechanisms: Resources are reserved hop-by-hop on the path between two communicating entities, sender and receiver. In STII, the sender issues a reservation request, specifying the traffic parameters called *flow-spec* and the associated QoS parameters. The request is sent across the network destined to the receiver, with resources reserved for the request along the path. Instead of the sender-initiated reservation approach of STII, RSVP is a receiver oriented protocol, where the receiver requests reservation as response to the sender's advertisement. The reservation request is carried backwards to the sender, while reserving resources on the returning path. The reservation is established when all intermediate network nodes reserve the required resource successfully; if any node fails to reserve the requested resource in the process, the reservation is aborted as a whole.

Despite existing reservation protocols' ability to support single-stream transport and playback, they fail to address the problem in the presence of multiple multimedia streams. In many multimedia presentations and documents, multimedia objects are not isolated; instead, they are related with each other both temporally and spatially [1, 8, 9]. The MHEG standard under development by ISO's Multimedia Hypermedia Expert Group also defines a correlation structure among multimedia objects [10]. Due to the temporal structure among multimedia objects, resource requirement varies at different stages during the lifetime of a presentation. This poses a challenge on the resource management system since so far resource reservation cannot handle sessions whose resource requirement change over the session's duration. In addition, the increasingly distributed nature of multimedia objects (such as in video-on-demand and multimedia Web document) further complicates the problem by involving the interconnecting network. We characterize this class of multimedia applications as Synchronized Distributed Multimedia Sessions (SDMS).

The network and system support for the transport and playback of multiple temporally-related multimedia streams is largely unaddressed. The existing reservation protocols cannot efficiently support the temporal structure on resource requirement imposed by SDMS. The existing reservation protocols mentioned above are of an immediate nature, where resource is occupied immediately after the reservation operation. This is not suitable for SDMS. If each multimedia stream requests for its own resource reservation just prior to its scheduled start time, the possible reservation failure will violate the temporal integrity of the session. Alternately, if all resources involved in the session are reserved before the entire session starts, reserved resources for non-immediate multimedia streams are wasted till their actual presentation time. The simultaneous reservation of all resources also implies a higher failure probability.

In this paper, we introduce a resource reservation scheme for SDMS based on the notion of advance resource reservations. The idea of advance reservations eliminates the temporal coupling between resource reservation and resource execution that exists in immediate reservation protocols. Resources are reserved for an specified temporal interval in the future. Advance reservation was initially proposed as an attempt to address the problem of resource reservation failure in situations such as multiparty video conferencing [7, 13]. In such scenarios, the unpredictable failure can cause the conference to be rescheduled, leading to many inconveniences for remotely located participants. Even if a reservation is retried later after a reservation failure, there is no guarantee that the reservation request will succeed. Reserving resources in advance solves the problem; in case a reservation attempt for a specific time is turned down, it can be rescheduled to a different time without affecting the participants. In this paper, we propose a resource reservation scheme for SDMS that can schedule a feasible session starting time, if one exists, and reserve resources accordingly. The scheme solves both temporal-correlated resource reservation problem and resource scheduling problem for multiple synchronized resource requirements.

The paper is organized as follows. Section 2 formally describes synchronized distributed multimedia sessions and its resource implications. Section 3 presents a resource reservation scheme. Section 4 describes the temporal interval intersection finding algorithm used in the scheme and the handling of concurrent reservations. After discussing some related issues in Section 5, Section 6 concludes the paper and lists some future research directions.

2. Synchronization distributed multimedia sessions

The most direct way to describe the temporal relationships among multimedia objects is through visual representations. There are a number of visual models to describe temporal relations among multimedia objects, such as Petri-Net [1, 9] and time-line [9, 10]. Figure 1 shows an example of a petri-net representation. The temporal relationship is defined based on the synchronization points. We use the explicit temporal intervals in our definition of SDMS, to be independent of the representation model. The intervals can easily be extracted from these models using simple algorithms.

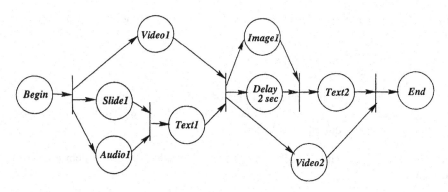

Figure 1.   A petri-net synchronization representation.

Definition 2.1. A Multimedia Environment (MME) is a 6-tuple, MME $= (O_e, Q_e, E, E_o, R, R_o)$, where,

O_e—Set of Multimedia Objects; including movies, video clips, sound waves, etc.

Q_e—Domain of Presentation Quality; for video, this contains the available values for parameters like frame per second, resolution and the number of DCT coefficients which controls the compressed video quality.

E—Set of End-Systems; An end-system is defined as either the producer (source) or the consumer (destination) of multimedia objects.

E_o—Location Function: $O_e \to E$; defines the source of each multimedia object.

R—The Resource Pool; contains resource associated with intermediate routers, switches and end-systems. Since resources are to be reserved in advance, there is a temporal interval associated with each resources reservation.

R_o—Resource Requirement Mapping: $O_e \times Q_e \times E \times I \to 2^R$; where I is the set of temporal intervals. The mapping defines the resource requirement (a subset of R) for transporting and presenting a multimedia object from its source to an end-system with a certain quality for a certain interval of time.

Definition 2.2. Given a Multimedia Environment, a Synchronized Distributed Multimedia Session (SDMS) is a triple, SDMS $= (O_s, I_s, Q_s)$, where

$O_s \subseteq O_e$—Set of Multimedia Objects for presentation in the SDMS.

I_s—Relative Presentation Interval Function: $O_s \to I$; where I is the set of intervals as before. This defines the object's presentation interval with respect to the session start time.

Q_s—Quality Function: $O_s \to Q_e$; specifies the presentation quality of each multimedia object in the session.

Let the session starts at time t, the absolute presentation interval of object o can be calculated by shifting the relative interval $I_s(o)$ by time t, which we denoted as $I_s(o) + t$. Note that the resource requirement for a session is the aggregate resource requirements from all the multimedia objects in the session.

Definition 2.3. The Resource Requirement for a SDMS starting at time t on end-system e, is

$$\mathcal{R}(e, t) = \bigcup_{o \in O_s} R_o(o, Q_s(o), e, I_s(o) + t).$$

Let $\mathcal{R}' \subseteq R$ be the resource already allocated in the multimedia environment. The following defines the notion of *Feasible Session Start Time*, a time that the session can start with all the resource requirement satisfied.

Definition 2.4. A Feasible Session Start Time for a SDMS on end-system e is a time t satisfying

$$\mathcal{R}(e, t) \cup \mathcal{R}' \subseteq R.$$

1. Client c sends *Object Reservation Request* for all objects to their sources. That is, for each object identifier $o \in O_s$, c sends objects reservation request with parameters $(o, I_s(o), Q_s(o), c)$ to the source $E(o)$ of the object.
2. When a source (called server) s receives the object reservation request with parameters (o, i, q, c),

   2.1. s determines the resource requirement for transporting and presenting object o with quality q for the temporal interval i to destination c as $R_o(o, q, c, i)$.
   2.2. s sends the *Resource Inquiry Request* for the resource requirement computed in 2.1 to the resource managers for each resource involved.

3. For each resource manager that receives the resource inquiry request, it checks its own resource reservation table and sends back to the original client c the *Start Times Intervals* for which the requested resource is available.
4. When client c gets back all the responses of resource inquiry requests from resource managers, it runs the *Interval Intersection Finding Algorithm* to find a start time that all resource requirements can be satisfied.

   4.1. If no intersection is found, it returns FAIL to the application.
   4.2. If a start time is found, it sends back to the resource managers the confirmation message with the calculated start time to confirm the reservation. And returns the start time to the application.

5. When resource managers receive the reservation confirmation messages, they modify their resource reservation tables to mark the resources as reserved.

Figure 2.   The resource reservation protocol.

In the next section, we will present a resource reservation scheme that schedules a feasible session start time and reserves resource accordingly.

3.   The resource reservation scheme

The entire reservation is logically a single action, although it involves multiple resources with time-correlations. Thus, either all resources are reserved or none is reserved. Let end-system (client) c issue a reservation request for a SDMS $= (O_s, I_s, Q_s)$, in the multimedia environment MME $= (O_e, Q_e, E, E_o, R, R_o)$, the reservation protocol shown in figure 2 is executed. A message flow diagram of the protocol is shown in figure 3.

We explain a few points about the protocol in more detail. The resource requirement is determined by the server in step 2.1 and contains both network and end-system resources. The request on each resource is associated with a temporal interval which is based on presentation interval in the multimedia session definition. Network resource requests are typically expressed in terms of traffic descriptors and QoS parameters requested. End-to-end parameters are broken down into parameters concerning individual routers and switches along the path.

As the resource requests are propagated over the network, there may be some resources, particularly network switches and routers that can get multiple resource inquiry requests from the same multimedia session. When this situation occurs, the resource manager should treat them as a single request. This is due to the possibility that they may be satisfied individually but have conflict with each other. A mechanism can be easily devised to achieve this aggregation of requests on the same resource from the same multimedia session.

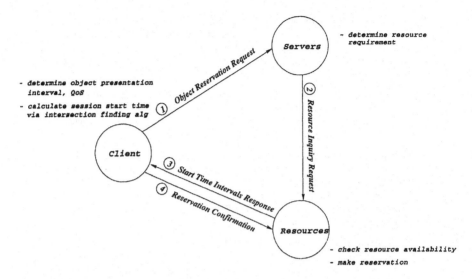

Figure 3.   Diagram of the resource reservation protocol.

The presentation intervals are defined with respect to the session start time, so is the resource requirement calculation in step 2.1. When the resource manager receives the resource inquiry request, it maps the received request into its reservation table and finds the possible places along the time-axis that the request can fit in. These places on the time-axis in turn decide the set of session start times for the requested resource to be available, referred to as start time intervals. Note that start time intervals are not intervals when the resources are available, but rather the set of session start times such that the required resources is available. Figure 4 gives an illustrative example of resource inquiry request and how the resource manager computes the start time intervals. In the example, a resource request is measured against the current resource allocation. Places that the request can fit in the available resource pool are determined, and the corresponding session start times are recorded as start time intervals. For different resource managers, the resource allocation strategy and thus the computation for start time intervals can be very different, depending on the specific resource allocation and scheduling techniques. Capacity-based allocation as shown in figure 3 is only for illustrative purpose.

4.   Intersection finding and concurrency handling

4.1.   *The interval intersection finding algorithm*

In response to a resource inquiry request, a resource manager computes and sends to the client the start time intervals, which is defined to be the set of session start times such that the requested resource is available. According to the definition in Section 2, a feasible session start time is a session start time such that all resources are available. Therefore, t is a feasible session start time if and only if t belongs to the intersection of the interval sets generated by all the resources involved. Figure 5 presents the algorithm.

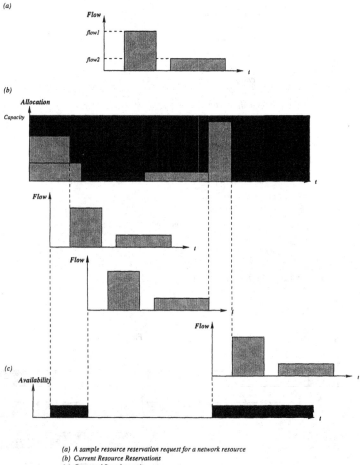

(a) A sample resource reservation request for a network resource
(b) Current Resource Reservations
(c) Computed Start Intervals

Figure 4.   An example of resource request and start interval computation.

We assume all intervals are closed and all indices start from 0. N is the number of resources, $I[i]$ is the number of intervals of resource i, and $B[i, j]$, $E[i, j]$ denote the end-points of the jth start time interval of resource i, respectively. The algorithm uses T to keep track of the current candidate intersection point and $C[i]$ and $T[i]$ to maintain the current interval and candidate intersection on resource i, respectively.

Figure 6 shows a running instance of the algorithm on a sample set of intervals. Basically, the algorithm is a time-axis walk, leaping only through the starting points of intervals. The algorithm loops through the set of resources, during each iteration it checks the current T against the intervals from the resource under inspection, determines a new T before stepping to the next resource. Once the same intersection is encountered a second time, the intersection is found and it is the current T. In the example, T is initially set to the starting point of the first interval of resource a. The algorithm goes on to check resource b, finds out that T does not belong to an interval of resource b, thus T is incremented to the starting

```
function Intersection
    T ← B [0, 0]
    for k ← 0 to N − 1 do
        C[k] ← 0
        T[k] ← −1
    end for
    i ← 1
    while TRUE do
        if T = T[i] return T
        j ← C[i]
        while (E[i, j] < T) do
            if j < I[i] − 1 then j ← j + 1
            else return FAIL
        C[i] ← j
        T ← max(B[i, j], T)
        T[i] ← T
        i ← (i + 1) mod N
    end while
end
```

Figure 5.   The interval intersection finding algorithm.

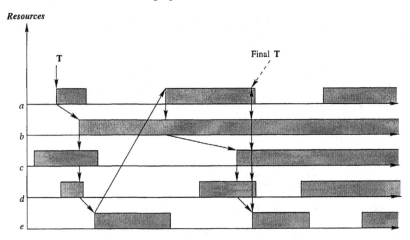

Figure 6.   An example of time-axis walk in the insection finding algorithm.

point of the next interval of resource b. As the algorithm steps through resources c and d, T falls in their intervals and therefore does not change. Resource e cause T to be incremented again since T does not belong to its intervals. After inspecting e, the algorithm loops back to resource a. The procedure continues until T (as pointed by the final T) goes through resources a, b, c, d, e and back to a again without any change, when it is returned as the intersection and the algorithm terminates.

The structure of the algorithm is simple and straightforward. Using the same notations as above, the algorithm uses $O(N)$ space in addition to the storage for input data. The worst case running time is $O(N\Sigma I(i))$, where $\Sigma I(i)$ is the number of intervals. Even in the worst case, the running time is acceptable. With a hundred resources each generating a hundred intervals, the running time is in the order of tens of a millisecond on an ordinary workstation. The following two alternative schemes further reduces the running time. The first is an early-start scheme to reduce the reservation latency by taking advantage of the time-monotonic run-time structure of the algorithm. In particular, instead of letting all intervals be sent back from the resource at the same time after they are computed, we allow intervals to be sent back individually as they are computed. This parallelizes the interval generating at the resource side and the intersection finding at the client side. It can be particularly useful when the resources are slow in generating intervals, for example, because some complicated admission control tests are used. Similarly, on the client side, instead of starting the algorithm when all intervals are received, we start the algorithm as soon as the first interval arrives. The execution can only be blocked by an attempted inspection of an interval not yet arrived. Eventually, one of the following two situations will occur: an intersection is found, when the algorithm sends a stop message to cancel the ongoing interval generations by the resources and ends its execution; or the algorithm fails to find an intersection, and a fail is returned.

The distributed nature of the reservation procedure enables another variation—the early-intersection scheme. In the original protocol, intervals are only intersected at the client site after they are received. Considering the fact that the resources a session requests lie on the paths from the client to the multimedia servers, we can let the intermediate node calculate the intersections as the intervals are carried over the network. Here, the intersections are defined as intervals rather than points. Each node receives a set of intervals from each of its upstream node, intersects them with the set of intervals generated by itself, and sends the resulting intersections to the downstream node. The intersection algorithm at each node runs in linear time with respect to the number of intervals (each node has fixed number of upstream nodes). The scheme reduces the overall computation time by distributing intersection computation to participating nodes. The early-intersection scheme can easily be combined with the early-start scheme, where intersections are calculated at each node and sent downstream one by one.

4.2. Concurrent reservation handling

Due to the distributed nature of resource reservation, concurrent reservations need to be handled carefully. In immediate reservations, if two reservation requests cause conflict on some resource, one of them simply aborts. In our scheme, because of the advance nature of reservations, we can adjust the session start time so that the next attempt may succeed.

Consider two separate resource reservation requests, A and B. A issues the request and gets back the intervals from resource r. B does the same thing. A and B find their start times separately by running the intersection finding algorithm, and then send the reservation confirmation messages to the resources. However, if the start times they found happen to conflict with each other on some resource, then at least one confirmation is going to fail. This could happen because there is no way to tell whether two requests will have resource conflicts before the intersection finding algorithm calculates the session start time. Also a resource manager cannot commit the resource when it receives the inquiry request, since the time required to reserve the resource is not known until the session start time is calculated.

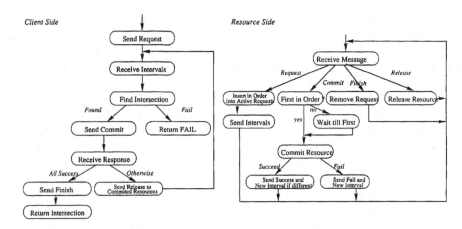

Figure 7.   Partially ordered concurrency handling technique.

We can use a technique similar to concurrent transaction processing in distributed database management systems to address the problem. An ordering is defined on the set of requests, using timestamps or any other criteria. Each resource manager keeps a queue, according to the ordering, of all requests that are waiting to commit their requested resource. Commit requests are executed in the queued order. The commit operation of a request not at the head of the queue is blocked until it becomes the head. Notice that the requests are only "partially ordered", in the sense that only requests active at the same resource at the same time are ordered. Upon commit failure, the resource manager will regenerate the intervals. The client will calculate a new intersection time and the commit operation is attempted again. Figure 7 shows the procedure. By using the technique, all satisfiable reservation requests will eventually succeed despite the possibility of temporary resource conflicts.

5.   Related issues

5.1.   Resource management

Local resource managers need to provide resource management services to the reservation protocol. This set of services constitute an abstracted resource layer, upon which the resource reservation protocol is based.

- *Resource inquiry.* Given a resource request, the local resource manager should be able to generate temporal intervals during which the resource requested is available. For implementation purpose, the system can define an upper bound on how far into the future an advance reservation is allowed, which in turn poses a limit on the number of generated intervals. Usually, some kind of admission control is used in generating temporal intervals.
- *Resource reservation commit.* The resource manager should be able to commit the resource reservation, record the committed resource and the corresponding time interval

in its reservation table. Admission control is involved.

- *Resource reservation release.* Release resource from the reservation. Delete the corresponding entry in the reservation table.
- *Resource scheduling.* Schedule incoming service units at run-time to meet the committed QoS from reservation. It is not a interface service, but rather an internal mechanism to commit the promise by the interface services.

5.2. Resource requirements: QoS mapping vs. QoS provisioning

With regard to the relationship between application level QoS and resource requirements, many proposals have taken the approach of QoS mapping. Applications run a QoS mapping algorithm that translates application level QoS parameters into resource level requirements. Resource reservation requests are then issued for the required resources.

In a distributed environment, the mapping from the application level QoS to resource level requirements might not be static. In other words, a universal mapping function might not exist. In a remote video playback example, the resource required by a playback request is largely determined by the specific algorithms used by the video server. Techniques such as disk storage layout optimization, compression, temporal smoothing, statistical multiplexing and multicasting can all change the required resources for achieving the same application level quality. We adopt a more scalable QoS provisioning approach, in which the applications send their application level QoS requirements to the servers of the multimedia objects. The servers in turn determine the required resources depending on the requested presentation quality, based on the particular mechanisms they use.

Even with a given presentation quality, a server might still be able to adjust its *transmission schedule* that represents different tradeoffs among resource requirements. For example, with a large client buffer size, the video server can ask for a lower bandwidth by building up video buffer for a longer time before playback starts [11]. But with a small buffer size, the server may have to request a higher bandwidth to ensure on-time delivery of video frames. These kinds of tradeoffs on resource allocation can be taken into account by the server while generating transmission schedules, given resource availability information such as the client buffer and network bandwidth. In fact, making transmission scheduling decision is an integral part of resource allocation for SDMS. Once transmission schedule is determined, the resource requirements implied by the schedule can be reserved by the proposed resource reservation protocol. Good transmission schedule can enhance resource efficiency and reduce the probability of reservation failure.

5.3. Multimedia sessions in reality

A synchronized multimedia session is a deterministic and uninterrupted schedule of multimedia activities with a guaranteed quality. Many multimedia applications require these properties for inter-media synchronization and quality of presentation purposes. For example, applications may require individual multimedia streams start at exact time instants so that what is heard by the user corresponds to what appears on the screen. The requirement can easily be represented by a SDMS. Once a SDMS is defined, an application can take advantage of the resource reservation protocol to achieve the guaranteed quality presentation with the specified temporal requirements.

Some multimedia presentations have a fixed schedule among multimedia streams that can be treated as a single multimedia session. Other applications involving event-driven operations, for example, user interactions, may take different execution paths depending on the events received, thus having dynamic and unpredictable resource requirements. In such cases, two approaches can be taken: one is to calculate the minimum upper bound for resource requirements among all possible event-driven execution paths, and treat the entire process as a multimedia session. Then regardless of what path the application takes, resources are always guaranteed. The other approach is to cut the execution path at branching points and treat each component as a multimedia session. When an event is triggered, the application determines the next multimedia session and requests resources on the fly. There are tradeoffs between the two approaches. The former guarantees the timely behavior of the entire application, but may overbook resources; the latter does not waste resources, but the delay between successive sessions cannot be easily bounded.

6. Conclusion and future research

We have proposed a resource reservation scheme for synchronized distributed multimedia sessions. The scheme addresses the resource reservation problem of reserving multiple resources with temporal synchronization requirements, which is desired by a large class of multimedia applications with inherent temporal relationships among multimedia streams. By using resource inquiry and interval analysis techniques, the scheme not only can reserve the requested resources, but also schedule resource available times. This work can be extended in several ways. First, some multimedia applications have soft or elastic temporal relationships, where the temporal relationship among multimedia objects is not fixed but rather varies within certain constraints. How the proposed reservation scheme can be extended to handle the elasticity is an area of further study. Second, the scheme uses advance reservations which increases the resource management complexity, especially at reservation stage. Future work needs to be done to study and quantify the increased complexity.

Acknowledgments

This work was supported in part by the U.S. Department of the Army, Army Research Laboratory under Cooperative Agreement DAAL01-96-2-0002 Federated Laboratory ATIRP Consortium.

References

1. Y. Al-Salqan and C. Chang, "Temporal relations and synchronization agents," IEEE Multimedia, Vol. 3, No. 2, 1996.
2. R. Braden, D. Clark, and S. Shenker, "Integrated services in the internet architecture: An overview," Internet RFC 1633, June 1994.
3. R. Braden, L. Zhang, and S. Berson, "Resource reservation protocol (RSVP)—Version 1 functional specification," Internet Draft, Nov. 1996.

4. D. Clark, S. Shenker, and L. Zhang, "Supporting real-time application in an integrated services packet network: Architecture and mechanism," in Proceedings of the ACM SIGCOMM '92, 1992.
5. L. Delgrossi and L. Berger, "Internet stream protocol version 2 (ST2) protocol specification—Version ST2+," IETF RFC 1819, Aug. 1995.
6. L. Delgrossi, R. Herrtwich, C. Vogt, and L. Wolf, "Reservation protocols for internetworks: A comparison of STII and RSVP," in Proceedings of 4th International Workshop on Network and Operating System Support for Digital Audio and Video, 1993.
7. D. Ferrari, A. Gupta, and G. Ventre, "Distributed advance reservation of real-time connections," in Proceedings of 5th International Workshop on Network and Operating System Support for Digital Audio and Video, 1995.
8. L. Hardman, D. Bulterman, and G. Rossum, "The Amsterdam hypermedia model," Communications of the ACM, Vol. 37, No. 2, Feb. 1994.
9. N. Hirzalla, B. Falchuk, and A. Karmouch, "A temporal model for interactive multimedia scenarios," IEEE Multimedia, Vol. 2, No. 3, 1995.
10. T. Meyer-Boudnik and W. Effelsberg, "MHEG explained," IEEE Multimedia, Vol. 2, No. 1, 1995.
11. J.D. Salehi, Z.-L. Zhang, J.F. Kurose, and D. Towsley, "Supporting stored video: Reduce rate variability and end-to-end resource requirements through optimal smoothing," in Proceedings of ACM SIGMETRICS '96, 1996.
12. C. Topocic, "Experimental internet stream protocol version 2 (ST-II)," IETF RFC 1190, Oct. 1990.
13. L. Wolf, L. Delgrossi, R. Steinmetz, S. Schaller, and H. Wittig, "Issues of reserving resources in advance," in Proceedings of 5th International Workshop on Network and Operating System Support for Digital Audio and Video, 1995.
14. L. Zhang, S. Deering, D. Estrin, S. Shenker, and D. Zappala, "RSVP: A new resource reservation protocol," IEEE Network, Sept. 1993.

Wei Zhao is a Ph.D. candidate in Computer Science at the University of Maryland at College Park. He received his B.S. degree from FuDan University in Shanghai, China in 1989 and M.S. degree from the University of Maryland in 1996, both in Computer Science. His research interests include Network and OS Support for Distributed Multimedia and Quality of Service Architecture in Intergated Services Networks.

Satish K. Tripathi was born in the village Patna, District Faizabad (UP) on January 20, 1951. He attended the Banaras Hindu University and completed his B.Sc. and M.Sc. (Statistics) in 1968 and 1970. He stood first in both B.Sc. and M.Sc. in the university and obtained gold medals. He joined the Indian Statistical Institute, Calcutta to do research in Computer Science. In 1972, he left for Canada for higher studies and attended the University of

Alberta and the University of Toronto, obtaining Ph.D. in Computer Science from the University of Toronto. Dr. Tripathi joined the Computer Science faculty at the University of Maryland in 1978. He served as the Department chair during 1988–1995. In March 1997, Dr. Tripathi joined the University of California at Riverside as the Dean of Engineering and the Johnson Professor of Engineering. For the last twenty years Dr. Tripathi has been actively involved in research related to performance evaluation, networks, real-time systems and fault tolerance. He has more than hundred papers in international journals and refereed conferences. In the networking area, his current projects are on mobile computing, ATM networks, and operating systems support for multimedia information. He has supervised more than 15 Ph.D. dissertations. Dr. Tripathi has served as the member of the Program Committee and Program Chairman for various international conferences. He has guest edited special issues of many journals and serves on the editorial boards of Theoretical Computer Science, ACM/Springer Multimedia Systems, IEEE/ACM Transactions on Networking, International Journal of High Speed Networking, and IEEE Transactions on Computers. He has edited books in the areas of performance evaluation and parallel computing. Dr. Tripathi is a fellow of IEEE.